MICHIGAN POW CAMPS
IN WORLD WAR II

GREGORY D. SUMNER

THE
History
PRESS

Published by The History Press
Charleston, SC
www.historypress.net

First published 2018

Manufactured in the United States

ISBN 9781625858375

Library of Congress Control Number: 2018948031

For John Baxter,
Renaissance Man

and

Hannah Arendt, Heinrich Böll, Carlo Levi and Primo Levi,
Germans and Italians whose humanity knew no boundaries

CONTENTS

CONTENTS

ACKNOWLEDGEMENTS

The best thing about researching this book was the excuse it gave me to travel around the four corners of the beautiful state of Michigan—including my first trip to the fabled U.P. I met kind and helpful people all along the way and am indebted to those associated with the public libraries and local historical societies who do such important work in preserving our heritage.

I also thank the staffs at the National Archives in Washington, the University of Detroit Mercy Library, the Hatcher Graduate Library at the University of Michigan and the Walter Reuther Archives at Wayne State.

Special thanks to Emily Foster for sharing her stories about the POWs she knew during World War II, as well as Larry Carter, Chris Causley, James Conway, Kathy Cyr, Omar Doran, Leona Foster, Yarleth Gomez, Brenda Lyndyke, Bob Myers, Howard Poole and Joan Thompson.

I also much appreciate the people at The History Press for making my second book with them a smooth and enjoyable process—especially Laurie Krill, my editor, who always went the extra mile, and Abigail Fleming, my gifted and dedicated copyeditor.

A shout out to Alexandra Hichel at UDM for her wizardry with the photographs.

Thanks, as always, to my wise and supportive agent, Robert Thixton.

And love to my family and the friends who gave me extra encouragement on this project, including Casey Blake, Ron Carpenter, the Tuesday Night

ACKNOWLEDGEMENTS

Goldfish gang, Commissioner Roy Finkenbine, Amy Howes, Donald Kroger, Marty Leever, Eric Mesko, Maryrose Patrick, the Recchias, Dan Rosbury, Battle Captain Robert Rouse, Sigrid Streit, Jim Wheeler, Mike Wilhelm and the rest of the Mingoes, the Wilberts and Logan, Alexandra, Lucas and Isaac.

"A BREAK FOR THE UNDERDOG"

MICHIGAN'S WORLD WAR II POW CAMPS

Emily Foster brought them back with crystal clarity: those late summer and early fall days of World War II, now seven decades distant, when German soldiers came to work on her family's acreage in the heart of Michigan's bountiful Fruit Belt. Over tea in her living room that July Saturday in 2016, Mrs. Foster recalled to me how, as "a naive country girl," she marveled at the exotic visitors and, in spite of barriers of language and rules against "fraternization," could not help but get to know them as human beings—in her words, "big brothers."

The stories poured forth that afternoon—oft-told, perhaps, but with a sincerity and good humor that was infectious. Looking back, she considered those men—pawns in a game of grand strategy and global warfare—as no less than a "deliverance," the answer to her father's prayers at a time when hands for the harvest were in desperately short supply. Without them, the better part of three bumper crop years of apples, peaches, apricots and cherries would have been left to rot in the fields.

Emily spoke with special fondness of the first group of POWs. Their youth concealed the fact that they were professional soldiers from Rommel's Afrika Korps, men who had endured the indignity of defeat and surrender after months of hard fighting in the desert. With thousands of their German and Italian cousins, they had been herded into cages and stockades, shipped across the Atlantic and then taken by rail across prairie and mountain to holding camps in a country whose vastness defied the imagination.

If the prisoners Emily encountered were any indication, efforts by the War Department to weed out incorrigible Nazis and Fascists in their ranks were having considerable success. These fellows were unfailingly correct and polite in their behavior, and they were willing to work long hours without complaint. Many (though by no means all) were actually relieved to be out of the war. When asked about their hopes for the day when peace returned, the response was, to a man, simple and timeless: to return *home*, to be reunited with their loved ones after a long and painful separation.

Emily explained to me the dilemma her father, William Teichman, faced in the summer of 1943 as the American part of the war rolled through its second year. Tire and gas rationing meant that the Arkansas families who usually worked Michigan's orchards were not able to make the trip. When a notice appeared in the local paper announcing that POWs at the new fairgrounds camp near Sodus, twenty miles north, could be contracted to fill the gap, Mr. Teichman seized the opportunity, requesting a detail of ten— the minimum allowed.

Soon men with "PW" marked on their backs became a common sight in Berrien County, bouncing along in the back of the flatbed trucks that carried them to and from their work assignments. They seemed in good spirits, singing and waving to people along the way. The single American MP assigned to guard them, clearly a man of more "advanced" years, sat in the passenger seat, paying them little mind as he dozed or daydreamed.

Though the majority of the residents of that part of southwestern Michigan were proudly German in ancestry, few understood more than fragments of their grandparents' language. "You *will* speak English, and you will speak it *without* an accent," Emily remembers her aunt sternly insisting. Her father, a veteran of the Great War, was an exception to the rule, and in addition to being pressed into duty as a translator for neighbors who had also taken on POW labor, his fluency allowed him an unusual rapport with the men under his supervision. The bonds only deepened once he convinced Sodus officials to assign him a regular group, eliminating the need for constant re-training in the basics of thinning and picking fruit.

Each workday around noon, Mr. Teichman brought the prisoners to the front yard for their lunch break. As a twelve-year-old, Emily's job was to set up tubs of clean water so they could wash off the dust of the morning and organize packing crates so they could sit with at least a degree of comfort. Her father ate his meal outside with them, under a shade tree, while the guard—"a real *character*," she recalled with a smile—joined the rest of the family inside at the kitchen table.

Lunchtime at the Teichman farm during World War II. The child in the photograph is Emily's younger sister Judy. *Courtesy of Berrien County Historical Society.*

Emily's mother, Leone, noticed that the bag lunches provided to the prisoners—usually a slice of hard salami wedged between stale crusts of bread—were hardly appealing, let alone filling, and they came without proper utensils. The men deserved better, so she made it her business each day to work up a homemade dish for them, maybe chili or spaghetti, to be washed down with coffee or a cold glass of lemonade.

In her mind, this was nothing special, just a bit of the hospitality people who lived in the country were used to offering their guests, including strangers, as a matter of course. The expressions of gratitude on the faces of the men, however—still familiar to Emily even today—showed that they felt otherwise. The ritual was repeated, again and again, over three summers.

Emily shared her best anecdotes about the Germans, some light and comic, all wonderfully revealing. She remembered, for instance, the prisoners' astonishment when her father encouraged them to eat any ripened fruit they came across on the ground—it was no good for the market anyway. Some had not tasted a peach in years. There were the Sunday-afternoon soccer matches, intensely competitive but full of joshing and boisterous laughter. And then there was the gentle way the men played with her younger siblings during their free time. Some had not interacted with children for years—including, in many cases, their own—and they clearly missed its spontaneous joys.

Mrs. Foster recalled for me Franz, a paratrooper and an accomplished equestrian in civilian life, who patiently worked with her late afternoons as she refined her riding technique. When a barking dog spooked her mount one day, causing a fall, Mr. Teichman invited the German medic inside to tend to his daughter's leg, which he did with easy confidence and skill. When a prisoner lost his footing on a ladder in a stand of cherry trees, her father rushed him to the family doctor in Eau Claire for treatment, rather than driving him—as prescribed—all the way back to base camp.

A stickler for doing things "by the book," the Sodus commandant would have been outraged by these departures from protocol, of a kind no doubt happening on farms throughout the county—had he known about them. But thanks to an unspoken conspiracy of silence, he was kept in the dark, and in any case his reprimands were objects of fun easily dismissed.

The guard assigned to the Teichman farm was all by himself "a walking violation," Emily observed, prone to sneaking in naps and occasionally misplacing his helmet and rifle. It didn't matter. "They weren't *going* anywhere," she insisted, chuckling at the obviousness of the point.

She laughed again when remembering the day a cloud of dirt appeared on the horizon as the commander's jeep hurtled, unannounced, toward the house. Her father was away at the time, but Emily knew exactly what to do, dashing out to the barn, bridling her horse and riding to the orchards in a Paul Revere gallop to alert her new friends about the "surprise inspection" on the way.

Today, the phrase *prisoner of war* evokes the specter of an irredeemably evil adversary connected to shadowy "terrorist" groups rather than nation states. Post-9/11 POWs are to be locked down and quarantined as far from public view as possible, consigned to twilight places like Guantanamo, where "enhanced interrogation" is allowed and the norms of civilized behavior don't always necessarily apply.

It has not always been that way, however, as Emily Foster's vivid testimony reminds us. The story of how, during the (admittedly very different) days of the Second World War, this nation attempted to live up to the letter and spirit of the Geneva Convention Relative to the Treatment of Prisoners of War—in contrast to its opponents, and even its allies, notably the Soviet Union—is a case in point. It is a chapter of our history that deserves to

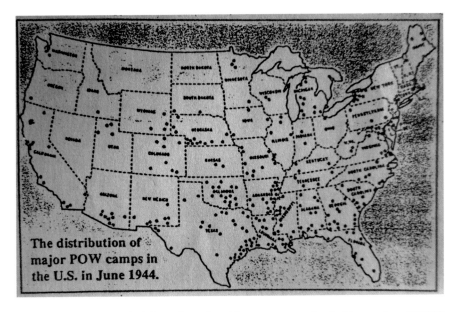

The distribution of major POW camps in the U.S. in June 1944.

The War Department administered a nationwide camp system that held more than 400,000 POWs from 1943 to 1946. *Courtesy of the National Archives.*

be retold and celebrated, as an expression of the democratic values young Americans were risking and giving their lives around the world to defend.

Even "good wars" are messy, of course, and Uncle Sam's record in this area was far from spotless. Abuses, atrocities and vigilante-style reprisals are a fact of life in every combat zone, and where the fighting was fiercest, American GIs sometimes shot any figure they saw in field gray, even if he had his hands up. But for the majority of the 3 million Axis troops captured in the campaigns of North Africa and Western Europe, humane conditions were the standard. This was especially true for the roughly 425,000 POWs—mostly Germans, but also 51,000 Italians—held in more than five hundred camps scattered across the continental United States between 1943 and 1946.

Over six thousand of these men spent time in Michigan, housed in thirty-two base and branch camps in mostly remote corners of the state. Little physical evidence remains of most of these compounds, but newspaper accounts and experiences preserved in diaries and letters and interviews survive to reveal just how remarkable this "on-the-fly" wartime experiment really was. The rank and file of internees, the focus of this book, overwhelmingly remembered their stateside living conditions as clean

13

and safe, their food as abundant and healthful, the rules under which they operated tough, but fair. Reflecting on his time at Fort Custer, Konrad Kreiten observed, with massive understatement: "Such was not always the case for Americans taken prisoner overseas."

POWs were encouraged to volunteer for work assignments, as permitted by international law. The majority accepted the opportunities with enthusiasm, as they were a way to earn spending money for the camp PX and to simply pass the time. As Mrs. Foster understood, the men *were* a deliverance for Michigan's fruit growers, canneries, farmers and pulpwood producers. It is estimated that in 1944, POWs constituted *one-third* of the state's agricultural labor force. The Italians living at Detroit's Fort Wayne were kept busy, meanwhile, maintaining city parks and playgrounds, upgrading municipal buildings, resurfacing streets and the like. Prisoners made their presence felt in other ways, too, inside and outside of the camps, drawing on their widely varied talents. As a historian of Fort Custer has written, "They came from many occupations, from hardened soldiers, auto mechanics, carpenters, to opera singers."

In the course of their employment, the POWs often developed relations of friendship and even family with the Americans they met. The "no fraternization" policy made sense in theory and on paper, but in practice it was impossible to enforce, as we see in the example of young Emily and her adopted "brothers."

The fact that German Americans like the Teichmans populated so much of rural and small-town Michigan (with roots dating back as far as the 1830s) and that large Italian American communities lived in the state's industrial centers and in the mining and logging country of the Upper Peninsula surely helped to make this kind of exchange possible. Hildegard Sailer recalled how her husband "immediately recognized" the dialect spoken by Otto Zwick, a POW working on their Monroe County farm. It was the one spoken in his boyhood home in Bavaria. A letter from another prisoner thanking the Kent County family who had been so kind to him during the war conveys the circumstances well: "We were only a couple generation away from the sail boats which brought us here."

In short, it made a *difference* that right below the Croswell *Sanilac Jeffersonian* headline "Prisoner of War Camp Established at Airport" was a notice announcing "Schutzlers Observe 45th Anniversary."

And the bonds, once formed, endured.

To be sure, not everyone welcomed these "enemies in their midst," and things did not always go smoothly. Some civilians voiced opposition to the

Efforts to quarantine POWs from contact with civilians were probably doomed to failure. *Courtesy of the Michigan Military and Technical Historical Society (MMTHS).*

program based on security concerns, while others grumbled about what they imagined to be (based on rumor, rather than reality) the "coddling" of the internees. People in every community needed time to adjust to their new neighbors. But with familiarity, suspicion almost always evolved into trust and mutual respect

Bullying was not uncommon behind the barbed wire, instigated by a small but hard-shell minority—in some (necessarily rough) estimates perhaps 10 percent of the POW population—who sought to impose their version of party discipline on their fellow prisoners. A larger number continued to profess loyalty to cause and Führer to the bitter end—or at least went through the motions. It was, after all, not easy to turn one's back on a lifetime of indoctrination, and there were few, if any, overnight conversions to the enlightened Yankee values of pluralism and civil liberties. News of each setback for the Axis caused morale to sag. Accidents, slowdowns, even small-scale sabotage occurred at work sites, and a few internees even made attempts to escape. The scourges of worry, boredom and homesickness, along with the strain of being watched, however loosely, by uniformed men brandishing guns, weighed on every prisoner as the war dragged on and on.

But most of the men cooperated with their custodians or at least tried to meet them halfway. They avoided challenges to minimum security and emerged from the experience grateful for the way they had been handled. When they left for home, they carried back with them a sense of admiration for their host country, with many expressing their determination to return one day to become citizens. This was a claim, as Melissa Amateis Marsh notes, "no Allied [prisoner] in a German *stalag* or a Japanese POW camp would ever make."

Like the national program, Michigan's POW system must be judged a success, a bright spot even in the shadow of a terrible world conflagration. In August 1944, the editors of *Collier's* magazine set forth the animating principle, the thing that made it all work so well:

> *We ought to be humane and generous in this matter, because we are Americans, and because we believe as a nation in decency, humanity, humaneness and a break for the underdog, which the prisoners surely are.*

PART I

STRANGERS IN A STRANGE LAND

CAPTIVITY

No one doubted in 1943 that the road to victory in Europe for America and its allies remained a long and bloody one. As events unfolded that pivotal year, however, the tide was turning, perhaps decisively, in the right direction. The Nazis' earlier *blitzkrieg* triumphs faded into memory as Hitler's over-extended air, naval and ground forces met reversals on every front. In January came the last act of the disaster in the frozen ruins of Stalingrad for his once invincible *Wehrmacht*, followed by an agonizing retreat as the Russians seized the initiative in the east.

By spring, meanwhile, what began as Operation Torch in occupied North Africa reached the mopping-up stage as grizzled Tommies and green Yanks finally overwhelmed their German and Italian counterparts in the sands of Libya and Tunisia. The gaze of strategists in Washington and London now turned northward, to landings in Sicily and beyond.

Hardcore Nazis and Fascists swept up in those desert campaigns remained defiant even as they lay down their weapons, keeping faith in ultimate success for the Axis in spite of present difficulties. For the less ideological, however—especially draftees and enlisted men—the attitude was more complex. Heinrich Böll described it well when he wrote of the "strange state of simultaneous liberation and imprisonment" a man enters when he becomes a prisoner of war. Many admitted to feelings of euphoria at having been providentially delivered from a doomed cause. As they thrust hands into the air and began the journey into captivity, they allowed themselves the thought, for perhaps the first time, that now

Success on the battlefield, like the one described in this paper from a community in Michigan's Upper Peninsula, presented new challenges to Allied war planners. *Courtesy of MMTHS.*

they were going to survive the war in one piece. "I was completely glad to be captured!" remembered Virgilio Razzo in Louis Keefer's oral history *Italian Prisoners of War in America.* "It was one of the happiest days of my life. I didn't want to be in it in the first place!"

The sentiment spread with each defeat in each new theater of battle. In *An Army at Dawn*, Rick Atkinson recounts how some American units in Sicily

An endless procession of POWs snakes it way through the North African desert, 1943. *Courtesy of the National Archives.*

were so overwhelmed by Italians abandoning Mussolini that they had to post signs reading: "NO PRISONERS TAKEN HERE."

"You can't work up a good hate against soldiers who are surrendering to you so fast you have to take them by appointment," quipped combat cartoonist-at-large Bill Mauldin. To his eye, the hundreds of prisoners "crowded into great clumps among the dunes" gave the scene "something of a Coney Island look."

Germans were not immune to the temptations of giving up, either. Private Ernst Floeter recalled his joy at being rounded up in Normandy in the weeks just after D-day. "I threw my rifle down, happy that my wish had come true."

For some men, the transition into noncombatant status came with adrenaline and fireworks, just like in the movies. For most, however, the end came quietly. "I had always imagined a highly dramatic scene, and it was nothing of the kind," Franco di Bello observed of the day he and his *compaesani* complied with shouts of *mani in alto!* from a British Eighth Army recon patrol. From there on, di Bello remembered, "[e]verything was so plain and common, that, emotionally, I felt very let down."

As a group, the prisoners taken in North Africa were a battered lot, not surprising for men long deprived of food, fuel and ammunition and plagued by fleas and mosquitos and dehydration in 120-degree daytime heat. Many displayed the vacant thousand-yard stare of shell shock after

Germans surrendered by the tens of thousands in the frozen winter of 1944–45. *Courtesy of the National Archives.*

weeks of near-continuous artillery and mortar fire and the strafing of American P-38s and British Spitfires. When they crossed over to Allied lines, they were confronted with evidence of just how badly the crusade on which they had been sent was going. "Why in the devil haven't those guys already won the war?" Ottone Grego recalled thinking as he shuffled, at gunpoint, past rows of gleaming new Sherman tanks parked to the horizon. Provisions and equipment by the ton lay stacked everywhere, at the enemy's disposal—and more was arriving every day.

General Eisenhower put the word out down the chain of command that as far as prisoners of war were concerned, the United States would strictly observe the rules set forth in the Geneva Convention of 1929, to which it was a signatory. Allied planes dropped leaflets that spelled out in multiple languages how those who chose to surrender would be protected. Over Ike's signature, the fliers declared:

The soldier who carries this [safe-conduct pass] *is using it as a sign of his genuine wish to give himself up. He is to be disarmed, to be well looked-after, to receive food and medical attention as required, and to be removed from the danger zone as soon as possible.*

The document was intended to counter the warnings given Germans and Italians at the front that they would face torture or even summary execution once in enemy hands. Some saw it as a trick, while others took comfort in its reassurances.

Atkinson describes in all its color the menagerie that was channeled, on foot and in all manner of vehicles, to the open-air stockades hastily erected to serve as temporary quarters. Cultural and class differences were on full display, the rule of thumb being the higher the rank the cleaner the uniform and the more theatrical the capitulation. Here, in the grimmest of monochrome landscapes, passed a spectacle worthy of comic opera:

The prisoners came by the hundreds, then the thousands, then the tens of thousands...waving white flags made of mosquito netting or their underwear. They came in neat columns of field gray, singing "Lili Marlene" with that annoying German trick of clipping the last note of each line. They came as a bedraggled mob of mangiatori, *singing sad Neopolitan* [sic] *ballads, or in sauntering platoons of Italian paratroopers, overcoats draped on their shoulders like the jackets of* boulevardiers *on the Via Veneto. They came in dun-colored Afrika Korps trucks with palm tree insignia stenciled on the tailgates; or in alcohol-burning buses piled high with baggage and pet dogs; or in chauffeured Mercedes sedans, colonels and generals dressed in gorgeous uniforms with Iron Crosses at their throats and boots so beautifully buffed that, as one GI said, "you would have thought the bastards were going to a wedding."*

The rank and file made little trouble as they were moved from one holding area to another. Observing the columns as they passed by, Americans and Brits took due satisfaction at the humbling of their adversaries—particularly the fearsome, "arrogant" Germans. "The *Herrenvolk*, like chickens in a yard," remarked one GI. Now they were reduced to scavenging for cigarette butts discarded on the parched ground.

For those who had imbibed "master race" theories, the African American MPs barking orders at them, in English, only added to the humiliation.

Preoccupied with more pressing strategic demands as the war moved ever forward, Anglo-American leaders devoted precious little thought to the job of taking care of prisoners—who, in any case, came in numbers much larger than expected. Over a matter of weeks in Tunisia, more than 200,000 flooded into facilities meant to accommodate perhaps 70,000. Their handling was therefore an ad hoc, disorganized affair, bordering on chaos in some places. And human nature being what it is, reports of abuse were not uncommon, in spite of protocols and monitoring. Vandals among the Arab population took advantage of the opportunities for profit and revenge suddenly presented to them, as did many French colonial officials.

Patterns of indiscipline among Allied troops ranged from degrees of harassment and violence to outright extortion and larceny. "Everything was placed in a pile from which the captors helped themselves," Arthur L. Smith Jr. observed of the process. "[A]t countless checkpoints along their odyssey," Ron Robin tells us, the vanquished found themselves "pounced-upon by triumphant American soldiers seeking souvenirs"—weapons, medals, pieces of uniform, wedding rings. "[T]he aggressiveness of the searchers heightened as the distance from the front increased." Their high value on the black market made cameras, eyeglasses and medical instruments especially prized as war booty. A German enlisted man recalled his despair at having been stripped of the symbols of his identity: "Where my national insignia was sewn there is now a hole through which my undershirt can be seen. On my wrist…is a band of white flesh where a short time ago my wristwatch kept the skin from becoming tanned."

Antonino Mineo remembered one guard in North Africa notorious for trading jewelry in exchange for ears of corn and other scraps. "We saw the bad Americans in that camp," he ruefully observed decades later. "We didn't see the good Americans until we got on the boat."

Not every POW endured such abuses, and there *were* good Americans to be found, even in the earliest stages of captivity. Journalist Ernie Pyle, who landed with U.S. troops as they established a beachhead near Gela, on the south coast of Sicily, described for his readers back home the high spirits and geniality of the Italians now suddenly out of the war: "They munched on biscuits, talked cheerfully to anyone who would listen to them, and asked their American guards for matches. As usual, the area immediately became full of stories about prisoners who had lived twenty years in Brooklyn and who came up grinning, asking how things were in dear old Flatbush."

Noting that the Italians in Sicily had met the invaders with "something less than ferocity," Bill Mauldin observed the same kind of post-surrender familiarity: "Most of them seemed to want to explain that they had kinfolks in Detroit."

Keefer offers the testimony of Samuel Buretta, an Italian American with Mauldin's Forty-Fifth U.S. Infantry Division who did everything he could to insure just treatment for the distant cousins in his charge:

> *It hurt me to see these men behind barbed wire, because I knew in my heart that they didn't want to fight us, and now only wanted to go home. So, while I had them, I put them to work in humane ways, such as working in hospitals, loading and unloading trucks, and so forth. I put my heart and soul into that job. When I saw them being cheated on rations, with bread and other staples being diverted [for] personal gain by others, I fought for them, and put a stop to the practice real fast!*

TO THE "LAND OF SOFT DRINKS AND CANNED FOOD"

Success on the battlefield left Allied leaders with a dilemma that went beyond the rounding-up process: what to do *next* with all these bodies, so suddenly fallen into their laps. The crowded holding pens, lacking even the most basic amenities, would have to do in the short term, but more permanent accommodations needed to be found or created—and *fast.*

At war now for four grueling years, Great Britain had neither the resources nor the space to absorb more than a few of the quarter-million prisoners already held on its island. The alternative that won the day was an example of the common-sense improvisation that was the hallmark of American thinking. Convoys of Liberty ships were making runs eastward across the Atlantic every week, loaded with men and materiel. Why not use their empty holds on the return trip to transport POWs, en masse, to the wide expanses of the United States? And once delivered, why not use them—within the rules of the Geneva Convention—to alleviate labor shortages plaguing the homefront? With his usual foresight, Army Chief of Staff George C. Marshall had suggested just such an idea as early as 1942. "[T]here would be a fine basis of employing these men," Marshall observed in a secret War Department memorandum, "perhaps in mines, on the beet fields and in similar work, possibly moving them by companies from crop to crop."

And so, on foot, in truck beds and cattle cars along jammed coastal roads or by water on rickety coal steamers, the prisoners were moved west to Oran, Algiers or Casablanca, en route to America—the fabled land of plenty, of "soft drinks and canned food without end," in the words of

Reinhold Pabel. There was often a stop in Liverpool or another English deep-sea port along the way.

Before each boarding, the cargo was counted and recounted, searched, interrogated, fingerprinted, catalogued and tagged. Judith Gansberg noted that the policy of routinely confiscating identification papers (*Soldbücher*) from German captives added unnecessary complications to the process. One by one, the medics poked and prodded the men, screened them for disease, injected them with vaccines and administered generous quantities of DDT powder that burned the skin on contact.

Officers and others with heightened intelligence value were taken by air to the United States. Others made the trip on converted ocean liners, now thoroughly stripped of their peacetime luxuries. Atkinson describes how, in the service of POW transport, even the *Queen Mary* was subjected to the indignities of streamlining:

> *Carpenters had removed any belowdecks fitting that could be used as a weapon, while installing alarm bells, locks, sandbagged machine-gun redoubts, and coiled barbed wire around dining and exercise areas. Now from deep in the hold came the drone of five thousand German prisoners, bagged in the North African campaign.... Three hundred British soldiers stood watch below.*

> *Any guard inclined to befriend the enemy was advised, "Remember their barbarities." In truth, five days of violent zigzagging across the North Atlantic had rendered the barbarians docile.*

Wounded prisoners were loaded with injured American servicemen onto specially equipped hospital ships. By all accounts, care was given to those who needed it without regard to nationality.

For the majority of captured troops—men from tank, infantry and air corps units, unaccustomed to the rigors of maritime travel—the voyage proved to be an ordeal. Sardined into vessels never intended for comfort, they held their stomachs and their breath as they rolled and tossed and turned though the rough seas. John Van Roekel conveys the misery of the experience in his novel *Prisoner Moon*:

> [T]*he* Mitchell *returned to the United States with nine hundred German prisoners. The bunks in the holds stood six-high, so tightly packed that if there was a man in the bunk above him,* [one] *couldn't roll over from his*

back to his stomach without having to slide out first. Barbed wire had been welded across the portholes.

In addition to overcrowding, stale air and a diet of cold C-rations, prisoners would recall for the rest of their lives the confusion and disorientation they felt on their passage to the New World. Anxiety haunted fitful attempts at sleep, and in their forced idleness, dark rumors swirled about where the ships were headed.

The heavy-handed security on board only fueled the prisoners' fears. Americans had little experience in handling POWs bound for the States. Fewer than two thousand were shipped from the western front during the First World War—and they weren't taking any chances this time around. "[T]he sentries are armed with machine guns and rifles, at the ready, loaded, and the safeties off!!!" Aldo Ferraresi wrote in his diary, the words dripping with indignation. "Are they afraid of a mutiny, or that we might jump in the ocean?"

After what seemed an interminable span of time, the convoys reached the ports of Boston, New York or Norfolk, Virginia. Despite the news blackout requested by Washington, the arrival of so many POWs could hardly be kept secret. Civilians lined the docks to ogle as the prisoners filed down gangplanks, calling out to them (mostly) friendly greetings. Then followed hot showers, a stop at the delousing station and another round of medical exams.

Each prisoner was allowed to keep his uniform, or what was left of it, properly cleaned and fumigated, and could wear it on the grounds of the camp to which he was eventually assigned. Beyond the barbed wire, however, dark green or blue denim fatigues with the big letters PW stenciled on the back, sleeves and pants would be the mandatory dress. Some were able to keep at least a few personal items, despite the gauntlets of looters and souvenir-seekers they had to negotiate after capture. Ernst Floeter convinced a sympathetic guard to retrieve his confiscated good-luck charm, which he credited with seeing him through the rest of the war.

As Kevin Hall has noted, the internees, arriving at the rate of thirty thousand a month by 1944, experienced surprise bordering on shock at the bustling activity everywhere apparent in their ports of debarkation. Like millions before them, those who passed through New York's harbor regarded with awe the sleek, enormous skyscrapers, seeing in them the mythic country of limitless horizons they had learned about from movies and magazines. Garishly lit by European standards, America's coastal cities had not, as the

Ships jammed with POWs bound for America ply the rough seas of the North Atlantic.
Courtesy of the National Archives.

propaganda led them to believe, been reduced to rubble and dust. Was it a
trick—"some sort of Hollywood illusion," perhaps, as one POW speculated?
No—not even the Yanks, famous for their engineering genius, could have
rebuilt everything so quickly and completely. Once again, the evidence

in front of their eyes raised troubling questions about Axis prospects for victory. "Our morale could not become worse" recalled one German of the initiation process.

The next leg of the journey was by rail, as POWs were dispersed to far-flung camps and military bases all across the United States. They rode in Pullman cars, on seats threadbare due to wartime austerity but otherwise impossibly plush compared to the military transports to which they were accustomed. Michigan-bound Konrad Kreiten recalled his amazement when black porters entered his car and began serving the prisoners coffee, bread and jam. The rich food made some men sick, but it was a welcome signal that perhaps the days of extreme hunger were over. Each POW was issued his own kit containing a towel, soap, toothpaste and a toothbrush. "We felt that we were in paradise," Kreitan remembered, "[and] had become again humans." Never mind the heavy iron bars outside the windows.

On the way west, many no doubt expected to see the rough-hewn gunslingers, noble native warriors and vast buffalo herds depicted in the romance stories of Karl May they read as children. More than anything, it

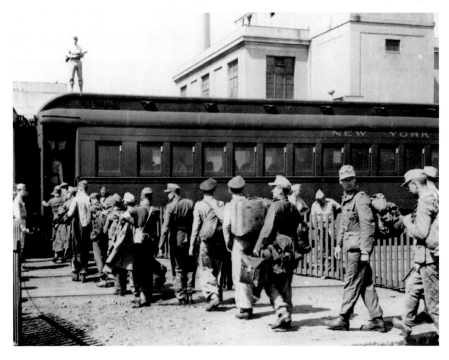

Under tight security, German prisoners board a train in Boston. *Courtesy of the National Archives.*

was the sheer *scale* of this alien landscape that was hard to digest. "We have been driven around in circles," one Afrika Korps skeptic reassured his mates.

In his novel *Wolf's Mouth,* John Smolens imagines for us the thoughts of Francesco Giuseppe Verdi, an Italian infantry captain bound for somewhere in a vague abstraction known as the Midwest. The time it took his train to go from Boston to Chicago was "a revelation," Verdi remembers, longer than required to traverse the entire length of his country, from Torino to Bari. And America's prodigious dimensions were matched by the apparent wealth of its inhabitants: "There was an incredible amount of farmland, so much that the Po River valley would be lost in a state such as Michigan. I had never seen so many cars; they were substantial and well-made, but the remarkable thing was that most of them appeared to be owned by ordinary citizens."

Verdi detects flaws in this dream world of abundance, however: "Houses were typically constructed of wood, and many were poorly maintained. Stone and brick were reserved for city buildings—town halls and post offices. These…lacked any sense of proportion and were uglier than anything Mussolini's architects had designed."

Perhaps the war *was* lost to this Colossus, but there was something missing, a permanence and solidity Verdi associated with home. "America could not last," he mused to himself, "because it was built out of wood."

Whatever creature comforts the POWs enjoyed on their journey, they were still headed toward an uncertain fate, and keeping up morale remained a steady challenge. "You think you're a tragic case?" a soldier in *Prisoner Moon* asks his despondent friend, en route to Ann Arbor:

> *Everybody on this train has a sad story to tell. Perhaps the American airplanes have bombed your family out of their home. You haven't heard from your pregnant wife for many months. We're all on our way to some miserable prisoner-of-war camp. In America!*

Others, like Floeter, were more hopeful about what was to come. He took in the passing scene with the eyes of a tourist hungry for adventure:

> *On this trip through America, I kept a log of all the cities and rivers we traveled past or crossed, including the mileage. Other guys were playing cards or sleeping all day long. I couldn't understand why they didn't care where they were going. They had the chance of a lifetime to see something new.*

Among the sights that most impressed Floeter was Dearborn's Ford Rotunda, visible as his train made its way through the western outskirts of Detroit. In its modernist grandeur it reminded him of Centennial Hall, an engineering landmark in Breslau he had once visited in his long-ago civilian days.

LAUNCHING THE MICHIGAN EXPERIMENT

The regions of the South and Southwest, with their mild winters and lower maintenance costs, were at first deemed the most logical places in which to establish America's POW camps. But government and commercial interests in the Great Plains and Great Lakes lobbied in Washington to get their fair share, too. Millions of men from these areas were away in uniform, after all, and many of those left behind were employed (for reasons of high wages as well as patriotism) in the munitions plants. Housewives and high school students were recruited to help bridge the labor gap, but there were simply not enough of them to eliminate the problem.

Michigan was near the top of the list in terms of in need. Famous for its industrial might—Detroit was the epicenter of the "Arsenal of Democracy," a network of wartime mass production that included Pontiac, Flint, Saginaw, Lansing, Grand Rapids and other communities—the Wolverine State has always been a major producer of agricultural products as well, and there were not enough hands to get the job done. The crisis was much the same in the lumber country of the Upper Peninsula—the fictional Captain Verdi's destination.

The Michigan POW program began on September 27, 1943, when a trainload of 374 Germans and 170 guards from Fort Grant, north of Chicago, arrived at the station in Benton Harbor, a lakefront city in the southwestern corner of the state. A crowd was gathered outside as the men stepped off the cars, duffel bags slung over their shoulders. Duane Ernest Miller gives us the curt observation of a *Benton Harbor News-Palladium* reporter who covered the

Benton Harbor Naval Armory, 2016. *Photo by the author.*

event: "They happen to be prisoners instead of conquerors. They are in luck or out of luck, depending on the point of view." Housed at the naval reserve armory, they were brought in to pick grapes headed for Welch's and other processing plants. With their good manners and their dedication to work, the prisoners quickly won the favor of the people who employed them.

In October, many in the group were transferred east to Caro, in the thumb region of the state's "Sugar Bowl." The Michigan Sugar Company had contracted with the U.S. Army to have POWs harvest sugar beets, which were in exceptionally high demand due to the rationing of cane sugar. The men would supplement and replace Mexican and Jamaican migrants about to depart the area. "[T]he southerners have wanted to go back to their homes with the coming of the colder weather," the *Tuscola County Advertiser* explained to its readers. "As a consequence, the employment of prisoners has appeared to be the only solution."

The arrival in Caro prompted the same hullabaloo as the one in Benton Harbor. Supervised by MPs and a detachment of the Michigan State Police, they were driven by truck to quarters at the county fairground on the west side of town. Lieutenant Patrick Whelen, the camp commander, "made it plain that the public will not be allowed to communicate [with them] in any way," it was reported. Enforcing the directive would be another matter.

The job proved physically demanding—"backbreaking," in the words of one German—and its methods took some time to master. But again, the results met and even exceeded expectations. "The prisoners are doing quite satisfactory work in the beet fields," the *Advertiser* observed, noteworthy "considering the fact that many of them had not done any manual labor since being captured in North Africa late last spring. Sore muscles in the arms resulted from first efforts, which responded to treatment in the camp infirmary." The POWs became an unremarkable sight as they commuted to and from the fairground each workday.

The success of the Benton Harbor and Caro pilot programs convinced the War Department to expand the Michigan experiment, opening it to locations statewide. Now POWs in large numbers began arriving to spend the winter at Fort Custer, the sprawling army facility that would serve as headquarters for the entire system.

PART II
FRITZ RITZ?

A QUESTION OF HONOR

Don't believe for a minute the rumor stories circulating today that we are treating our prisoners of war as prima donnas. *There is no pampering of the* German [at] *Fort Custer...and there is no bullying, no slave driving on the part of the men charged with guarding them.*

—Battle Creek Enquirer and News, *February 17, 1944*

Named after Michigan's famously star-crossed cavalry hero, Michigan's Camp Custer was established as part of the U.S. Army's mobilization for the First World War in 1917. Amid gently rolling hills straddling Calhoun and Kalamazoo Counties west of Battle Creek, it sits midway between Detroit and Chicago, making it an ideal place to induct and train young men from the Midwest on their way to becoming doughboys in France. In the 1930s, its neglected barracks were repurposed to accommodate recruits for FDR's Civilian Conservation Corps. With a new war looming in 1940, the compound, now Fort Custer, was expanded to fourteen thousand acres, its facilities upgraded for another generation of soldiers. Over the next five years, more than 300,000 uniformed Americans would pass through its gates.

Camp Custer's advantages of size and location also made it a natural choice as base camp for the German and Italian POWs who began arriving in the fall of 1943. The first order of business for administrators was to design a framework for the efficient handling of internees, no simple matter.

The catalogue of start-up challenges facing the Nebraska system described by Melissa Amateis Marsh applied to Michigan as well:

> *This meant…records sorted, typed and filed—a dozen times. This meant fingerprints, interviews, classification cards for assignment of labor. This meant counting heads in and out of the gate, checking thousands of work detail passes, emptying duffel bags, searching suitcases and frisking pockets for unauthorized articles that might facilitate escape. It meant handling of incoming and outgoing mail, censoring letters and forwarding personal property of PWs. It meant decisions, discipline, and a sense of direction.*

The prisoner-of-war division of the Army's Office of the Provost Marshal General (OPMG) in Washington issued guidelines for the layout and amenities expected of every camp across the country. Security came first, in the form of double barbed-wire fences enclosing the perimeter, in practice usually erected by advance teams of POWs. In accordance with the Geneva Convention, sleeping quarters and dining facilities for the prisoners were to be "equivalent to those furnished to United States troops."

Residents of barracks and dormitories were to have access to latrines, showers and laundry tubs, complete with "unlimited hot and cold running water." And recreation spaces were to be set aside, indoors and out, as well as a workshop, canteen, chapel and infirmary providing basic medical and dental care. In the smaller, seasonal tent camps, it was not possible to follow these specs to the letter, but every effort was made to conform to their spirit, as circumstances allowed.

Day-to-day management of the prisoners—getting them up in the morning, marching them off to the mess halls, overseeing worksite discipline and enforcing nightly curfews—was left largely to their own chain of command, beginning with the NCOs (noncommissioned officers, *Unteroffiziere*

POW Camps		
P1	Camp Allegan	
	Camp Evelyn	Ft. Custer (P9) was
P2	Camp AuTrain	the main POW Camp;
P3	Barryton	the other camps were
P4	Benton Harbor	temporary seasonal
P5	Blissfield	camps that were used
P6	Odessa Lakes	as needed. Many
	Caro	were former Civilian
P7	Coloma	Conservation Corps
P8	Croswell	(CCC) Camps.
P9	Fort Custer	
P10	Dundee	This is not a complete
P12	Freeland	list, it only contains
P13	Fremont	camps that we were
P14	Camp Germfask	able to find
P15	Grant	documentation on,
P16	Grosse Ile Township	there is evidence to
P17	Hart	suggest that small
P18	Camp Lake Odessa	groups of POW's
P19	Mattawan	were sent out to
P20	Mass	perform municipal
P21	Milan (USFR)	projects and were
P23	Camp Owosso	sometimes camped in
P24	Camp Pori	fields and parks for
P25	Camp Raco	short periods of time.
P26	Romulus Army Air Field	
		The issue becomes
P27	Shelby	even more cloudy
P28	Camp Sidnaw	with the Italian
P29	Sparta	Service Units as they
P30	Wayne (Fort)	were often afforded a
P31	Waterloo	greater range of
P32	Wetmore	freedom.

Michigan's thirty-two POW camps.
Courtesy of MMTHS.

to the Germans). Born of necessity, given the limited number of personnel available for security duty as well as language considerations, the arrangement worked well—so long as the people barking orders weren't ardent Nazis.

Decades later, Ernst Floeter remembered with gratitude the list of dos and don'ts— "especially the *don'ts*"— a veteran prisoner laid out to his group upon their arrival at Custer. The rules were no-nonsense and place-specific:

> [S]*tay ten feet from the fence because in the guard tower there are some trigger-happy Texans who have a sharp eye out for us; never, under heavy penalty, remove the screens from the windows; and be clean and shower daily. Anybody who got lice would be, in his words,* a Dreckschwein, *a "filthy pig."*

"We would now get to live in a clean environment," Floeter recalled thinking to himself with relief.

Intake procedures for each prisoner—which included an interview, yet more inoculations and a mug shot—were slow but on the whole orderly, a welcome improvement from the chaos attending the earlier stages of the captivity journey. "Everyone had a number," Floeter observed. "Mine was 31 G 72072. Now we were full-fledged prisoners of war."

U.S. troops abroad approved of the idea of adherence to the Geneva Convention—so long as it didn't take things too far. "Some very unfortunate rumors have drifted over here, from time to time, about the treatment of prisoners of war in America," observed Bill Mauldin, creator of the *Willie and Joe* cartoon "dogfaces." His words convey feelings held by many of those enduring the dangers and privations of front-line duty:

> *While the guys here realize it it much more economical to haul krauts back to the States on empty ships, rather than using crowded shipping space to send food over here for them, there is a natural resentment because the enemy gets a privilege that is denied those who fight him. He gets to go back and breathe the air of God's country, even if it is a prison camp. That's a very human and natural feeling, which can be fully understood only if you have experienced the deep longing for your home country that we have felt here.*

> *Since the Germans have many of our own men, and because we are supposed to be a civilized people, we certainly want the krauts to be treated within the rules, but only within the rules. [Emphasis added.]*

Besides perhaps leveraging at least marginally better conditions for Allied troops in Axis hands, there is evidence that America's commitment to fair treatment of POWs served to undermine the fighting spirit of its adversaries in the field. This was the rationale behind the safe-conduct leaflets that were air-dropped behind enemy lines. "Word of the contented lot of German prisoners in the United States, reaching Nazi troops, has caused them to give up in droves," declared an editorial in the April 30, 1945 *Grand Rapids Press* cited by Antonio Thompson:

> [O]*ur surrender propaganda, dropped from the skies, has fallen on more willing ears because of our liberal interpretation of the terms of the Geneva Convention. Perhaps we have erred on the side of kindness, but thereby we may have helped to shorten the war and bring more American sons, husbands and fathers home safely.*

Whatever the program's practical effects, and in the face of harsh criticism from some quarters, officials at the War Department held firm to the idea that exercising humanity toward the captive enemy was simply the *right* thing to do for a nation committed the dignity of the individual—"a civilized people," in Mauldin's words. "The [Geneva Convention] is *law*," asserted Major General Archibald Lerch, and a disregard for its requirements would threaten "the place of honor and moral leadership that [the United States] has earned in the eyes of the world," lowering it "to the level of Japan, whose emissaries talked peace while its army went to war."

"*HOGAN'S HEROES* IN REVERSE"

A 1944 profile by Margaret Galbraith, a reporter for the *Midland Daily News*, preserves for us a snapshot of the living conditions typical for Michigan's POWs. Galbraith toured the seasonal compound near Freeland, on the banks of the Tittabawassee River in Saginaw County (now the site of the MBS/TriCity International Airport). Freeland was one of a cluster of camps established in the center of the state to provide manpower for the sugar beet harvest. (Others included Owosso, Midland, Alma and Lake Odessa in Ionia County.) The layout and amenities she saw during her guided tour seemed to her more than adequate for the needs of its internees, almost all of them Germans, and morale at the camp was correspondingly high. Stuart Frohm summarized what she observed:

> *There were 20 barracks, 75 feet long, plus two mess halls for approximately 700 POWs, a mess hall for American guards, and recreation rooms. (At its peak the camp would house 1,070 prisoners.) Barracks had heating stoves, overhead electric lights, and double-deck and single bunks. Barracks shelves and lockers held westerns, mysteries, and other American fiction, candy and American cigarettes bought in the post exchange. Pin-up pictures cut from magazines were above the bunks.*

To Galbraith, the single most striking thing about the Freeland POWs was their *youth*. Along with battle-hardened "elders" in their early to mid-twenties, mostly captured in North Africa, there were, she found, quite a number of seventeen-year-olds who did not have to bother with shaving. Perhaps one in five prisoners understood or spoke some English, and those with the most fluency were naturally appointed by the others to act as spokesmen and intermediaries with the camp administration.

A few Freeland internees boasted to her about about ties to the United States that predated the war. One said he had spent several years in Philadelphia and kept in touch with siblings living in Wisconsin. Another served in the New York National Guard.

Knowledge in the camp about the overseas situation was spotty and laced with sometimes wild speculation. A surprising number of the prisoners Galbraith questioned still believed the fatherland would win the war, in spite of mounting evidence to the contrary. Maybe the flying bombs and other ballyhooed "secret super-weapons" said to be in the Führer's pipeline would allow him to yet again shock the world and snatch victory from defeat.

What kind of people worked in Michigan's POW camps? With a world war raging on multiple fronts, homefront duties of this kind were considered low priority and low status. Many of the officers assigned to manage operations were at or near the end of their careers. And more often than not, the GIs transferred in as guards were there by default, chosen from those classified as unfit for combat. "They were usually COs [conscientious objectors] or Purple Hearts," Emily Foster told me. Marsh quoted Major Maxwell McKnight of the OMPG on the uninspiring pool of manpower available in the early days of the system: "We were pretty much dredging the bottom of the barrel. We had all kinds of kooks and wacky people." Over time, however, selection and training grew more rigorous and reports of gross negligence or abuse by security forces remained rare.

There was a big difference between the strict rules governing interactions with POWs and the actual practice. Melissa Amateis Marsh noted the army guidelines on the subject outlined in a booklet given to all camp personnel—terse commandments meant to foster an attitude of distance and vigilance. Among them:

> Do not try to gain information from Prisoners of War.

> Do not ever believe a Prisoner of War likes you; he does not.

> Do not think a PW will not escape if he can. He will.

> Do not talk to PWs except in the line of duty.

In fact, fraternization between guards and the men whose heads they counted twice a day was commonplace, in all kinds of small and often clandestine ways. The sense was that these were men like themselves, with the same gripes, sorrows and dreams, and the situation would be reversed if the fortunes of war had played out differently. Despite the language barrier (very few guards spoke more than a few words of German or Italian), they bantered all the time with their charges, exchanging cigarettes and sharing photos of girlfriends, wives and children with them on lunch breaks. Some gambled with the prisoners, or imbibed homemade schnapps or grappa with them in the evening. As trust—and yes, a spirit of friendship—steadily grew, the *minimum* in minimum security became more and more pronounced.

It was obvious to the POWs that most of the men watching them were not exactly "spit-and-polish" professional soldiers. "Many times we noticed that a G.I. did not take his hands out of his pockets while talking to an officer," Custer internee Alfred Schumucker told an interviewer. Schumucker was quick to add that sloppiness, sloth and cutting corners were not vices exclusive to Americans: "We are all human beings. There are good ones and bad ones, there are intelligent ones and there are dummies. That applied to the prisoners as well as the guards."

Tensions and misunderstandings were to be expected in the camp environment, and with the ready presence of weapons, accidents and close calls did occur from time to time. "War Prisoner Treated at Custer for Wound" reads an item in the August 11, 1944 *Battle Creek News and Enquirer*. An American officer at the Benton Harbor camp fired two bullets into the ground when prisoners were slow to fall in to formation. One ricocheted, hitting an internee in the elbow. The damage was, fortunately, minor. Generally speaking, guns became less of a threat as guards and prisoners got comfortable with one another, no longer "locked and loaded" as before. Some work details operated without supervision at all, armed or otherwise.

Tales of lax security, real and apocryphal, abounded. "I remember that once our guard gave us his gun, because we would show him how the German would shoulder arms, arms up, arms down, present arms etc.," recalled Konrad Kreitan. "He enjoyed looking at it." Lyle LeCronier never forgot the day a Camp Freeland MP handed over his Thompson submachine gun and asked him, at age ten, to keep an eye on a group of Germans working in a beet field.

The back-and-forth between curious children like LeCronier and the POWs was usually light and playful—but not always. Monroe youngsters

Ike and Reni Icoangeli recalled riding their bikes to the camp east of town one day in June 1944, on what they later proudly described as a "Nazi-hunting" mission. When they spotted prisoners cleaning ditches and mowing grass, they began firing marbles with slingshots they had crafted out of tree branches and inner tubes. "Some of them got mad as hell and started yelling at us in German," observed Ike, enjoying the thought forty years later. "We aimed for their ass, but hit 'em everywhere." A battle cry accompanied the boys' fusillade: "This is for our brothers!"—a reference to the older Icoangeli siblings in uniform overseas. "I was a good marble shooter," added Reni, equally unrepentant. "I had a whole lunch box full of them." Without any sense of urgency, the guard on duty approached the assailants and gave them a mild scolding, then walked away, grinning.

John Senn remembered the startling sight of POWs playing with wooden toy guns careless neighborhood children left lying about in the vicinity of their work site. "They even made *ta-ta-ta* sounds as they waved and pointed them." The guard was in on the spirit of the moment, laughing as he made no effort to intervene.

An MP at another Michigan camp presented rods, reels and bait to the Germans in his custody so they could fish in a nearby lake while he spent the afternoon in town with his girlfriend. "None of us tried to escape," a spokesman for the group assured an interviewer, "and when he came back we gave him some of [what] we had caught and cooked."

While the inmates weren't exactly "running the asylum," internee Paul Lohmann recalled the almost maternal concern the men in his group had for their often bungling minders. The guards "thought it foolish to follow us around with guns," Lohmann explained, and the prisoners reciprocated by covering for them whenever they could.

> *They were tired of the War and the Army and wanted to go home. Since many of the GIs enjoyed an active night life, they were always tired during the day. We were all very young then, and we talked mostly about girls. We fully understood their tired conditions and we hid them, so that they could sleep during the day. We warned them when the Sergeant of the Guard was approaching to check on them. We always made sure that our "SLEEPERS" were up on time. We were very organized.*

Gerd Lindemann recalled with amusement a prank he and his fellow Camp Lakewood prisoners pulled on their guard one afternoon. As he lay dozing, several Germans crept beside him, removed his rifle and hid the disassembled parts. Then they began lobbing pebbles at his helmet. "He woke up," Lindemann told the *Kalamazoo Gazette*, "and he was all shook up." Needless to say the ransom demanded was agreed to without protest. "So each of us got free cigarettes and a candy bar, and we gave the pieces back. But he couldn't put it back together, so we put it back together for him. It was *Hogan's Heroes* in reverse."

People in nearby communities answered the call when asked to support the American personnel stationed at the camps, who were almost as homesick as the POWs. Civilians donated furniture for MPs' quarters, took them into their homes for meals and organized USO-style mixers and holiday events to help with morale. "That the people of Caro and Tuscola County did a real job of entertaining the soldiers who guarded prisoners of war here is revealed by compliments from many places," the *Advertiser* reported in a typical item in December 1943. Contributions by the American Legion and proceeds from a scrap drive sponsored by area churches funded the opening of a servicemen's center downtown, and other individuals and organizations pitched in to make it suitable for relaxing and socializing:

> *The Gamble store presented the center with five dozen roses, and 40 employees of Caro State Hospital did yeoman work in cleaning up the premises and getting the place ready for occupancy. Postmaster Donald Ellwanger did the lettering on the windows and had a mail box placed in front for the convenience of the soldiers. The art class at the high school, directed by Miss Lucy Brooks, painted the windows.*

THE PRISONERS

The temptation was strong, at least at first, to lump the prison population of the camps into categories based on ethnic caricatures: stern, fanatical Germans, amiable and hapless Italians. According to Ron Robin, the latter actually "basked in their image as happy-go-lucky, reluctant soldiers," turning assumptions about barracks full of men who were "content...easy-going, sometimes sloppy, and always cheerful" to their advantage. They used them to reassure young women they encountered outside the barbed wire of their good intentions. "We're not fighters at all," went the line. "We're lovers!"

It was not all make-believe. Even if POWs were out of uniform, many observers claimed they could determine the men's nationalities by their body language and behavior. Louis Keefer offers the recollection of a sergeant assigned to guard a labor gang of Italians. He liked them and participated in their evening soccer and volleyball games:

> But well disciplined they were not....For example, if they were detailed to some little landscaping project, they would show up carrying their shovels, hoes, and rakes every which way, relaxed and laughing, and ready to have some fun at the work.

> If they'd been Germans, every tool would have been shouldered at precisely the same angle and the formation would have marched silently to the job at strictest attention.

Generalizations along these lines made a rough kind of sense, perhaps, but they obscured the diversity and individuality that existed among the internees with regard to age, rank, battlefield experience and political outlook, regardless of national origin.

Marsh tells us that the POWS came to America in three distinct waves. In 1943, the commandos of the Mediterranean theater arrived: Luftwaffe aces, Hermann Göring Panzergrenadiere, sailors and submariners of the Kriegsmarine and Italian Bersaglieri sharpshooters, identifiable with their plumed, wide-brimmed hats. At the time of their capture, Axis forces were still in control in many places, and victory for their side remained possible, if not inevitable.

Next came the thousands of (mostly) Germans who surrendered in Northwest Europe after D-day, a group more pessimistic about the war's ultimate outcome. The bad tidings they carried into the camps were hard for even irreconcilables to ignore. "One of the greatest shocks to a batch of all-out Nazi veterans of the *Afrika Korps* is to throw a new detail of prisoners from Normandy in with them," Fort Custer commandant E.F. Richter told the *Battle Creek News and Enquirer* in October 1944. "When they get from their own kind the news that the German army is reeling back across France, they are not so inclined to believe that all the news in American papers, all the broadcasts on American radio programs, are lies—all lies."

Finally, there were the remnants of Hitler's once grand Wehrmacht, gathered up in last-ditch battles from the Ardennes winter offensive ("The Bulge") to the endgame in Germany in the spring of 1945. Emily Foster described to me the deterioration in quality she saw in the men who came to her family's farm over three years: the first group notably more correct and soldierly than the last, who were ill-trained draftees or teenaged "Hitler Youth types" indoctrinated from the cradle into Nazi dogma.

In the fall of 1944, the *News and Enquirer* reported that Custer's German population even included "members of the Jewish race." In an interview, Rabbi Martin M. Perley admitted his surprise when he got the call to pay them a visit in their barracks. "I was flabbergasted. Jews in the 'mighty' Nazi army? To me, it sounded just too incredible to believe."

The army chaplain dutifully gathered up his prayer books and menorahs and went to see the group of two dozen, still in their field gray.

Most of them, I found, were half-Jews, drafted right out of concentration camps and absorbed into labor battalions as the Wehrmacht's shortage of bodies grew desperate. Some were in the service barely a week when they were captured near the expanding Allied beachheads in France.

The men enthusiastically scooped up the religious materials I had brought with me. All of them were anxious to get their processing completed and be assigned to some work.

Their presence confirmed Perley's suspicions about the overall direction of the war. "To me," he concluded, "these men, wearing German uniforms, [are] concrete and convincing evidence that Hitler ha[s] reached the end of his rope, and that Germany's days are numbered."

Gerd Lindemann's experience gives us another window into the complexities of Michigan's POW population. A tank commander who reported directly to General Rommel, Lindemann was knocked unconscious by an artillery shell in a Tunisian olive grove on May 11, 1943, and taken prisoner, he told a reporter for the *Kalamazoo Gazette*. After a stop in Casablanca for initial treatment, he was taken by ship across the Atlantic.

Lindemann underwent surgery for shrapnel wounds at a military hospital in Topeka, Kansas, and then he was transferred to Camp Carson in Colorado, home to a group of German officers of the "goose-stepping" type. "That didn't go over too big with me, saluting all day," he remembered, "so I volunteered for work." The decision bought him to Camp Lakeview in the orchard country of Allegan County, south of Grand Rapids.

As the new commander of the Lakewood POWs, Lindemann did his best to boost their spirits. "I told the guys we're here. You might as well make the most of it. Treat other people the way you want to be treated." The approach worked well, for awhile. "If there ever was a problem, we worked it out ourselves. If a guy didn't keep clean, he got the 'Holy Ghost'"—a ritual that involved rousting the offender from his bunk and carrying him outside for a bath.

Lindemann's benevolent leadership was soon challenged, however. "One day a group of POWs arrived who seemed different. They didn't want to work and [they] supported the Nazi cause." When the veterans broke into cheers in the mess hall at the news of the Normandy landings, the newcomers started a brawl. Were they Waffen-SS? "There was one way to find out," Lindemann explained. "I said, OK, give them the Holy Ghost." Tattoos under the right arm confirmed his suspicions, and the troublemakers were promptly returned to the higher security of Fort Custer. "[A]nd that," he said with a look of satisfaction, "took care of that."

Many who surrendered in German uniforms weren't even Germans—especially toward the end of the war. In *Wolf's Mouth*, Captain Verdi reports that there were Austrians, Czechs, Poles and Hungarians at Camp Au Train, some of them volunteers, some of them coerced into service by the forces that had invaded and occupied their homelands. There is even a displaced Russian in the mix. "He never laughed," Verdi says of the mysterious loner. "He only stared fiercely at the rest of us, as though he would kill us the first chance he got."

Such distinctions were lost on on their caretakers. "Americans," complains Adino, the only other Au Train Italian after another day of affronts to his Latin pride. "We're all 'krauts' to them." His theory about why the natives were so dense on the subject? "It's because of the bread, I tell you. They eat this white bread that's like cake, and they don't know one damned thing."

Antonio Thompson confirms the gist of Adino's grievance, if not its cause, in his study *German Men in Uniform*. "Little thought was given to the differences," Thompson notes:

> *Besides, what would it matter if Fritz or Hans came from Austria or Poland or was a Democratic Socialist or National Socialist? They were still German, still the enemy, and all Nazis.*

> *Aryan mythology aside, the prisoners came from across Europe and Asia. Brown-skinned and brown-eyed soldiers of every conceivable age mingled with the "Teutonic" blonde-haired blue-eyed "German" youth. Germans and non-Germans and Nazis and non-Nazis mixed with the ideologically unsuitable, socially undesirable, and physically and emotionally unreliable. Some of these warriors used to feed the Nazis' war machine had little or no grasp of the German language. While the Americans considered the German soldiers a homogeneous group, the men in German uniform always remained conscious of the distinction[s].*

Due to its urban setting and the makeup of its population, Fort Wayne was an aberration in the Michigan POW camp system. Named after Revolutionary War general "Mad" Anthony Wayne, the ninety-six-acre compound sits at at the foot of Livernois Avenue in southwest Detroit, occupying a bluff that served as a Native American burial ground for centuries. Its massive star-shaped brick enclosure, along with its moat, earth embankments, vaulted tunnels, officers' quarters, powder magazine and cannon (never fired in anger) date to before the Civil War. The location affords a commanding view of Canada, just across a mile-wide bend in the Detroit River, as well as the southern approaches to the city from Lake Erie. Thanks to WPA funding, many of the buildings were restored in the 1930s after a long period of neglect.

During World War II, Fort Wayne was used as an induction and training center and the world's largest motor depot, the way station through which every jeep, tank, truck and spare part manufactured in the Arsenal of Democracy passed on its way to various battlefronts. In 1943, a section of its barracks was converted into a home for Italian POWs processed through Custer, who were put to work as cooks and janitors and in construction road crews, on and off the camp grounds.

Guards were struck by the morale of the Fort Wayne internees—higher than that of the Germans, in their estimation—as they went about their jobs and enjoyed themselves during off hours. There were episodes of insubordination, and prisoners complained about the winter cold and how they were being bossed around all the time. But the frictions were minor in nature. Though staunchly patriotic and homesick for loved ones and the rhythms of life back in Piedmont, Tuscany or Calabria, most shared the conclusion that being captured and evacuated from the war zone was the luckiest break of their lives.

"COVERT BATTLEFIELDS"

S tereotypes also obscured the power struggles waged between cliques of prisoners in every camp. Judith Gansberg speaks of "covert battlefields": conflicts between the majority Germans and those of other nationalities, between officers and enlisted men, between front-line soldiers and rear-echelon personnel and between "true believers" and those more concerned with day-to-day survival than ideology. Custer's Major Richter understood the dangers the latter presented and tried to quash them from the start. "Whether all are Nazis or not I don't know," he told the *Enquirer and News* in February 1944. "They make no particular mention of their leanings and shortly after they arrived here in October, I issued a directive that they should shelve politics. So far they have obeyed it to the letter."

Those closer to barracks life knew that no edict from above would solve a problem so complex. Despite a multistage screening process, there *were* voracious Fascists and Nazis in every camp, thugs bent on enforcing their ideas of discipline on their fellow internees, such as the Waffen-SS men Gerd Lindemann encountered at Lakewood. They insisted on rituals of fidelity to the Italian imperial cause or the glory of the Third Reich—mess hall portraits of Il Duce or the Führer, swastika emblems, booming choruses of "Deutschland über alles" and "Sieg Heils" as the American flag was raised in the morning and lowered at dusk.

The pressures to stay in line went beyond symbols. As part of their low-intensity guerrilla warfare against their captors, the faithful ordered

This page and opposite: German prisoners at Fort Custer maintained the rituals of their military discipline. *Courtesy of Brenda Lyndyke, Historical Society of Battle Creek.*

slowdowns and strikes (punishable at most camps under the "No Work, No Eat" rule) and other forms of petty sabotage. They convened secret late-night meetings during which those guilty of cooperating too much, laboring too diligently or other such treasonous offenses, however minor, were identified and singled out for reprisal. Men were harassed, ambushed, beaten (in a more brutal version of the Holy Ghost treatment) and sometimes murdered (or forced to commit suicide) on the authority of these kangaroo courts.

The size of these hardcore cells, variable with each wave of new arrivals, remains a subject of debate even today. Gansberg cites one estimate that perhaps 10 to 15 percent of German enlisted men were Nazi loyalists. In any case, the prisoners' stonewalling demeanor, stiff-armed salutes and marching songs punctuated with hearty shouts of "Heil Hitler!" or "Viva Mussolini!" no doubt led authorities to exaggerate their influence.

Ron Robin concluded that, for many internees, these were more a matter of reverting to the reassuring habits of their military training, interrupted by the chaos of battle, surrender and transport to the United States. "The first thing that struck me as I entered Camp Hood, Texas," an Afrika Korps trooper later recalled, "was that German discipline re-created itself right away, with its orders, its commands. *I had come home.*"

The rank and file did what they were told and tried to avoid drawing attention to themselves. Others, like Captain Lindemann, were more outspoken in their resistance to the few who sought to intimidate the many, exposing and denouncing them and offering protection to their targets. When identified, violent incorrigibles in Michigan were transferred to one of several maximum-security "segregation" camps out of state, like the ones in Aliceville, Alabama, or Alva, Oklahoma—notorious as the "Devil's Islands" of the national POW system.

CODDLING?

In coordination with officials at Michigan State in East Lansing who administered the prisoner farm work program, Fort Custer decided where satellite camps were to be located and for how long. The issue naturally aroused passions, and there was plenty of heated "Not in My Back Yard" rhetoric in town hall meetings and the editorial pages of the local papers. In Washington, the War Department received hundreds of complaining letters and telegrams every week, more than a few of them demanding that enemy combatants face summary execution. The list of American dead and wounded published each morning fed the anger, ensuring that there would be no shortage of volunteers for firing squad duty should the need arise.

In every community, pains were taken to stem the sense of alarm many felt toward the outsiders—camp personnel as well as prisoners. Van Buren County correspondent Gene Herbener scolded naysayers in his regular column:

> *The soldiers who are frequenting Hartford's loop district are all American guards at the labor camp. Timid folks who have been worrying over what might happen when the German prisoners enjoy the freedom of the town are authoritatively advised that that isn't the way the thing is being done. They'll remain at the fairgrounds. That is what the high stockade fence and the guards are for.*

Others took a more measured approach in responding to skeptics. Residents of Owosso in Shiawassee County read in the May 24, 1944 *Argus-Press* that an allotment of 250 POWs would be moving into a tent city on the grounds of the auto speedway on M-21, five miles west of town—with more coming later. They would be accompanied, the paper reported, by "the proper quota of military police guards," a ratio then fixed at one for every seven internees. Lieutenant Colonel Milton Gearing of the Sixth Army Service Command in Detroit said this of the new neighbors:

> *Most of them are in their early twenties and are well behaved....Outwardly they appear much like our own boys. In fact, if they were dressed in American uniforms you couldn't tell the difference. They are all very happy that the war is over for them and that they are doing the work that they are doing. We never had any trouble with them, and the people of Owosso need not worry about having any trouble with them.*

The assessment proved correct. Out of a camp population ranging up to one thousand—since records were destroyed after the war, a precise accounting is impossible—there were, with notable exceptions, very few problems indeed. A government brochure offered potential employers guidance in managing the most likely ones to arise, as when a prisoner might protest, "This is not in the Geneva Convention" or "We don't do it this way in Germany." In the interest of maximum productivity, harsh treatment or anything that smacked of slave-driving should be avoided. This would be important for larger reasons as well, influencing the world that would emerge once the shooting stopped. "Let them remember you as a fair-minded American."

The major contractor for Camp Owosso labor was the W.R. Roach Canning Company. Aunt Jane's Foods Inc., near New Lothrop, was another, using prisoners on all three shifts of its cucumber-salting operation during harvest season. A posting in the *Argus-Press* made it clear that POWs also were available to individual farmers who made proper application to the county extension agent.

Charles Rose's experience with the Owosso men dispatched to his family's acreage during the war was typical. "I had two German prisoners—Wilhelm Glegrich and Willie Link—working on my farm all summer," he recalled to the *Flint Journal* in 1986. "They were great help. They would take off their shirts and do anything we wanted." The trust level was such that when

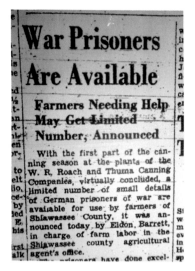

War Prisoners Are Available

Farmers Needing Help May Get Limited Number, Announced

With the first part of the canning season at the plants of the W. R. Roach and Thuma Canning Companies, virtually concluded, a limited number of small details of German prisoners of war are available for use by farmers of Shiawassee County, it was announced today by Eldon Barrett, in charge of farm labor in the Shiawassee county agricultural agent's office.

A notice to Shiawassee County farmers that POWs were available for contract labor. *Courtesy of Owosso Public Library.*

more laborers were needed, Rose sought their advice about who among their mates would make the best candidates.

Kenneth Schroeder had similarly positive memories of the prisoners who picked wheat, oats and sweet corn with him in 1945. "[That] summer my dad had three men, with no guard. We had the same three men every day, [and] I learned a lot from them. 42-year old Hubert Meyer spoke English and was a jack-of-all-trades." These were no Hitler loyalists, Schroeder understood after they shared their stories. "Hubert told dad…they were forced to fight with guns at their backs."

Schroeder noted the Germans' surprise that American farmers processed crops through an automatic threshing machine, a method they considered wasteful. "They went around picking up the grain that had been knocked out of the heads while being cut." Due to liability issues, internees were barred from operating such technology, but again—as was so often the case—the rule book was subject to flagrant everyday violations. The sight of a man in PW fatigues driving a combine or a tractor in Shiawassee County and elsewhere in Michigan attracted little notice as the rush was on to get the harvest in.

Generally, conditions at the Owosso Speedway camp were very good. The September 16, 1944 *Argus-Press* offers this folksy assessment of POW morale there:

> *They are a rather happy lot, despite the fact that they are prisoners, and go about their tasks whistling, singing and laughing. They do their work willingly and take exceptional pride in keeping the compound or stockade as neat as grandmother used to keep her parlor.*

The Germans at Owosso used scrap lumber to build floors under their tents as a barrier from moisture and the concrete slab foundation. "Occupants of one of the tents even went so far as to plant a small garden in front," the *Argus-Press* continued, observing that peas, squash and other vegetables, watered daily, were thriving. Everyone contributed his civilian

Prisoners at the Owosso Speedway camp line up for their pay coupons. *Courtesy of Owosso Public Library.*

talents—as carpenters, mechanics, cooks—to soften the surroundings and approximate the comforts of home. A beauty parlor operator from Berlin organized a barracks barbershop—which, as in the real world, served as a hub of social activity and gossip.

It is difficult for those of us who have not experienced prolonged episodes of hunger to appreciate the depth of the POWs' obsession with food. Germans and Italians alike had seen their caloric rations in North Africa reduced to the point where they had to fight, in the words of the *Battle Creek Enquirer and News*, "on little more than determination." As internees, visions of food appeared in dreams and waking life, and eating was always a primary topic of discussion out on the job and at evening bull sessions.

The POWs were grateful, of course, for the bread, cheese, sausages, pies and cakes the locals would sometimes pass to them through the fences. Smuggling occurred in full view of the guards, who looked the other way in exchange for their fair share of the contraband.

Unauthorized feeding of prisoners happened all the time at the work sites, as we know from Emily Foster's reminiscences of life on her Berrien County orchard farm. "The captain of the guard said not to feed them," Charlie Rose remembered of his experience with the Owosso POWs, but it was a hard rule to follow once families got to know the realities of the diet. "Each man was given two slices of bread and either a slice of meat or cheese for lunch. They had it eaten by 9:30 a.m. and were hungry by noon. So we asked them into our house and they ate lunch with us." Word of this kind of hospitality circulated in the camps, prompting intense competition for the prize assignments.

The outreach went the other direction as well. At first, Newaygo County residents gave a cold shoulder to the men of the tent town established there in May 1945. "The people of Grant were less than welcoming," the *Herald-Independence* bluntly admitted in a 1960 retrospective. "They were weary [*sic*] having enemies of their country so close to home, and their hostility transferred over to the military members stationed at the camp." Some 250 days of solid labor on area farms and in orchards and muck fields during the summer went a long way toward winning the locals over. What sealed the deal in warming camp/civilian relations, however, was a Sunday-afternoon chicken dinner held at the compound, advertised as free and open to the public. It was "a grand event, with food and song."

There were differences by nationality in the day-to-day fare at the POW compounds. The Italians' pasta creations—versions of the *pappardelle*, *tagliatella* and other staples they had grown up with—were especially popular with American personnel. "It looks like these foreigners take their cooking more seriously than we do," observed one satisfied MP on his way out of a Fort Wayne mess hall.

Barbed-wire chefs, Italian or German, had to operate under the same austere rules that governed civilian households, making the quality of their dishes all the more impressive. "It is strict Army policy," Croswell's *Sanilac Jeffersonian* assured its readers, "to cooperate with the national food conservation program by substituting on prisoners' menus foods which are plentiful and have a low ration point value."

Yanks expressed amazement at what could be done with the limited seasonings and meat sources at hand—-rabbit, the cheapest cuts of beef and pork, even Spam. And nothing, including the garbage, went to waste. "The first year they buried all [of it] in holes," Charlie Rose recalled of the Owosso Speedway camp. "By the second year the holes were filled up and the captain asked me if I could feed the garbage to my hogs. I said sure, and I went and got it every day or two."

Venison was another popular menu option for Michigan's POWs. John Pepin describes the teamwork and unorthodox hunting methods used to get it in the U.P.:

"It looks like these foreigners take their cooking more seriously than we do." Italian butchers show off their skills in the Fort Wayne mess kitchen. *Courtesy of Walter Reuther Archives.*

If one of the guards saw a deer during the day while on a woods detail he'd shoot it and gut it. Then later that night, guards would go back into the woods to get the deer with a dump truck. They unloaded it in an oil shed and the POWs would dress it out.

To get enough…for the entire camp, sometimes several deer would be shot with a Thompson gun, which could "drop a whole herd out there."

Though effective, this approach to putting dinner on the table was illegal. Conservation officers in the area made attempts to stop it—with mixed success.

The Germans' cuisine seemed less varied and less appealing than the Italians' to many camp personnel. "They prepared their food greasier than that [normally] served the U.S. soldiers," a Custer MP told Charles Marentette of the *News and Enquirer.* "Potatoes and large over-sized fried cakes were their favorite foods." Marentette noted that "[t]he eyes of American soldiers popped when they saw the Nazis at breakfast. Taking big strips of bacon, the Germans dipped it in hot water and ate it raw!" The prisoners were far from happy when Commander Richter, concerned about food poisoning, acted to ban the practice.

"German war prisoners at Hartford's fair grounds are said to prefer lard to butter," Gene Herbener commented on the camp diet, "which is all right with a lot of local butter eaters who have been short of butter and the red points with which to exercise their preference." Following a tour of the dining facilities with a visiting major from Fort Custer, Herbener could assure his readers that *no one* behind the fences was going hungry. "We never saw more appetizing roast beef and vegetables than were cooking on those army stoves." Staff, guards and POWs were all served exactly the same food—"[a]nd that includes butter," he added, tongue-in-cheek.

> *The Germans are not required to eat it, but it is placed before them. They would also prefer more potatoes and less meat. Meat has long been scarce in Germany and they haven't learned to like it. But any variations to please their appetites would not be following the Geneva rules, and America might be accused of non-compliance.*

"The only reason we didn't stay for mess," Herbener concludes in his profile, "was because the officers in charge forgot to invite us."

Perhaps as an expression of defiance, the German POWs drew lines whenever possible to make the camp diet conform to their tastes. "Spinach they eat with gusto, only after it has been ground to a fine pulp, mixed with mustard and nutmeg and dished out with a spoon," Marentette observed with the detached eye of an anthropologist.

> [Raw] *peanut butter was a surprise to them. And they complained that it stuck to the roof of the mouth. Mixing it with jam was a partial solution, but they still complain about "that stuff."*

> *Whole kernel corn—the tasty, golden kernels so highly prized in American kitchens—is looked upon with disgust by the Nazis who term it "swine food" and refuse any part of it.*

Germans at a Fort Custer mess table. *Courtesy of the Historical Society of Battle Creek.*

Dessert was a place of common ground, regardless of national origin. Every bit of kitchen ingenuity was needed to stretch and "make do" with ingredients that included precious little cane sugar. Margaret Galbraith lauded the Freeland bakers who "concocted a recipe for peanut-butter cake which [prisoners and] guards enjoy[ed] equally well."

Custer headquarters received sacks full of letters asking why enemy combatants feasted on hot chow every day while loved ones in the field overseas—Mauldin's *Willie and Joe* dogfaces—had to subsist on K-rations. Seeking to exploit the issue, one congressman regaled Washington wire service reporters with accounts of POW camp menus "typical of the Waldorf-Astoria."

Hyperbole aside, the fare *was* beyond the prisoners' fondest hopes, in both quantity and variety. "When the time came to eat, a whistle sounded and we were marched into the mess hall," Ernst Floeter recalled of his initiation to the dining regimen at Custer. "What a surprise! The tables were filled with food we hadn't seen in a very long time. We were urged to hurry up and get ready for seconds." By one estimate, German prisoners added an average of twenty to forty pounds to their battlefield-depleted bodies over the course of their time in the States. After visiting Allegan's Camp Lakewood, one journalist offered this assessment:

While there was never a "pot belly" nor a "hog jowl" to be found among the prisoners, neither were there the prominent ribs nor the hollow cheeks of starvation such as Allied prisoners had developed while interned under the Nazis. Generally the Axis soldiers held...in this country were lean, but it was the healthy leanness of regular hours, regular meals and lots of hard work.

In their correspondence, internees commonly instructed their families back in Europe *not* to send them packages of food so desperately needed at home.

Charges that POWs were being "pampered," "mollycoddled" or "treated like prima donnas" in Michigan and elsewhere across the United States had special resonance for the millions of citizens who, because of their race, were denied their right to equality, even as they made sacrifices to help win the war. Faced with the daily insults of Jim Crow in and out of the armed services, African Americans, Hispanics, Native Americans and other excluded people felt understandably betrayed when they were confronted with examples of preferential treatment for the enemy.

Tensions at Fort Lawton in Seattle over this issue made national news when they boiled over into a melee in August 1944. In a rush to judgment, twenty-eight black soldiers were court-martialed for the violence, which resulted in the death of an Italian POW, Guglielmo Olivotto. They were exonerated decades later for lack of evidence.

More typical was the experience of Lloyd Brown, an enlisted man turned away from a whites-only diner in Salinas, Kansas, with a group of fellow black troops stationed at the local army base. "You boys know we don't serve colored here," the owner told them as they walked in—with a nervous smile the first time, more firmly the second. "We ignored him," Brown said in an open letter he wrote to a newspaper about the incident, "and just stood there inside the door, staring at what we had come to see—the German prisoners of war who were having lunch at the counter." The rumors were true, after all. Brown remembered:

There were about ten of them.... They were dressed in fatigues and wore the distinctive high-peaked caps of Rommel's Afrika Korps. It was something we had to see with our own eyes. The Germans now had half-turned on their stools and were staring back at us, each man's cap at precisely the same cocky angle. Nothing further was said, and when the owner edged toward the phone on the wall we knew it was time to go.

David Carson Jr., a Michigan GI stationed at Camp Gordon in Georgia, witnessed a similar scene in a Texas train station snack bar. The Germans were "comfortably seated" inside, he recalled, "laughing, talking, making friends, with the waitresses at their beck and call. If I had tried to enter... the ever-present MPs would've busted my skull, a citizen-soldier of the United States." Testimonies like these appeared in the *Pittsburgh Courier*, *Chicago Defender*, *Michigan Chronicle* and other organs of the black press, and the hypocrisy they revealed was condemned as un-American from church pulpits across the nation, helping set the stage for postwar changes to the racial status quo.

In truth, despite nicknames like "Fritz Ritz," accommodations for the POWs in America were spartan. Konrad Kreitan likened Fort Custer to a large, "well-run boot camp." Time and again, reporters and even congressional investigators debunked charges of coddling to the satisfaction of most (but not all) who raised concerns about it. In acknowledging the lack of planning behind his crash housing program for the enemy combatants who began arriving in 1943, Maxwell McKnight summed up its bare-bones guiding principles: "Our whole concentration was, you build the damnedest and cheapest that you can for security purposes."

But guards and administrative personnel would long remember how the prisoners reacted when they first laid eyes on the quarters that had been prepared for them. "We were assigned to our barracks, which were really something," Custer POW Floeter recalled. "[A] shower and rest room in each one, very airy, and clean beds too." More than a few wept, shedding the tears of condemned men suddenly granted reprieve.

Soon enough, the routines of captivity would become second nature for them, from the bugler's jarring reveille at 5:30 every morning to lights out at precisely 10:00 p.m. every night. Complaints would come, rough edges would show and a gnawing sickness for home would never release its grip on these denizens of a world in limbo. But at least they were alive, out of harm's way and had the comfort of each other's company. Most successfully acclimated to their surroundings, understanding that there were worse ways to ride out the war.

RESPECT

The example of Camp Sparta, at the edge of a small town in the orchard country north of Grand Rapids, gives us a good sense of the relations that generally existed between POWs and civilians in Michigan. On July 31, 1944, the two hundred members of the Growers Association of Kent, Ottawa and Muskegon Counties, meeting in a warehouse west of town, voted unanimously to petition the State Extension Service in East Lansing for a contingent of prisoners to help with the area's critical labor shortage. The initiative was led by members of the prominent Kraft family, whose acreage bordered the appropriately named Fruit and Peach Ridge.

A month later, on August 31, a two-acre tent camp was set up out near Sparta's waste treatment plant. Four hundred German veterans of the North Africa campaigns were delivered the next day, fresh from bringing in the string bean crop near Remus. According to a report in the *Sentinel-Leader*, FBI agent Howard Bobbitt prepared the way for them, emphasizing in a Rotary Club talk that the POWs, mostly twenty to twenty-two years in age, should be considered soldiers rather than criminals, and thus presented no danger to the local populace. Things would go smoothly, just as they had elsewhere in Michigan, he assured the gathering of businessmen, if civilians exercised common sense and maintained their distance.

"The streets of Sparta were lined with people when we arrived" remembered George Loewe, one of the forty Americans assigned to guard the "Peach Ridge" POWs. It was a sign that Bobbitt's plea for distance would not be easy to enforce. One grower recalled:

Tent camp, Sparta, Michigan. *Courtesy of Larry Carter, Sparta Township Historical Society.*

That first year the prisoners were nice, bright, clean-cut fellows. They were big, husky and young, and just go, go, go all the time. They must have been the cream of the German army. They were so disciplined that there was never any quibbling about orders. Actually, the Army only sent a guard out here the first two days. Afterwards, the prisoners were on their own.

The Germans were predisposed to a less favorable impression of their hosts, "tend[ing] to regard Americans as being somewhat soft, too used to luxury, thus hedonistic and undisciplined," in the words of a profile in the *Grand Rapids Press.* "[B]ut [they] respected [the natives'] sincerity, ingenuity and ability to mobilize their country in a crisis situation."

"One of the things that surprised them was to see the owners working alongside their employees," Katheryn Ebers remembered of the prisoners assigned to her family's 450 acres. "Also, they were amazed at all the cars and trucks and by the fact that young children were driving them."

Eighteen-year-old Merlin Kraft, home thanks to an agricultural draft deferment, got to know many of the Germans during his days with them in the orchards, and he identified with their plight. "I could see they were defeated and sour," he recalled later. "How would you feel in another man's country? [T]hey were family men, husbands, fathers, boyfriends… boys, thousands of miles from home." One admitted that most nights he cried himself to sleep.

"They were all nice fellows," according to grower Welsey Mawby, "but some of them were real homesick. A few had pictures of their homes in Germany." Those who had been farmers spoke with pride of their patches of land and their bounty.

By the way, this kind of empathy with the enemy conformed with the national picture. A survey in 1944 found that three in four Americans blamed the Nazi leadership rather than the German citizens for the war.

Merlin Kraft was especially friendly with Roland Detshel, a leader and spokesman for the Peach Ridge internees, most of whom knew little English. From Detshel he learned that many of the men retained faith in victory for their side, believed the propaganda about their country as the benighted "land of beauty and of discipline" and "adored" still their General Rommel, "almost as a father-figure." As in other camps, there was a group of Nazis using Gestapo-like tactics to try to keep their fellow prisoners in line, but their numbers were small.

Detshel seemed to be somewhere in the middle. "I remember [he] and I would argue a lot about ideology," Kraft recalled, pausing to note that at this point the worst horrors of Hitler's regime had yet to be revealed. "[He said that] when Germany won the war he would ask for our farm and I could work for him. I was never sure if he was kidding or serious."

Echoing the sentiments of his neighbors, Kraft was struck by how fast the POWs learned what they were taught and how much effort they were willing to put into their labor assignments. "A hundred bushels of apples a day is considered a good day's picking," he explained. "We had one prisoner who consistently picked a hundred a day. When we asked him why he worked so hard, he said: 'So I can keep my mind off my wife and little girls.'"

After the war, Merlin Kraft kept an autograph book with the names and addresses of the Germans who had worked for his family. There were fond memories to preserve, like the time his mother baked a birthday cake for Heindrich Feldmen, embedding in it a silver coin he would find when he served it to his mates. Feldmen repaid the kindness a week later, presenting her with a ring expertly fashioned from the coin.

The Peach Ridge
POWs were known
for their hard work.
*Courtesy of Sparta
Township Historical
Society.*

Roland Detshel. "When Germany won the war, he would ask for our farm and I could work for him." *Courtesy of Sparta Township Historical Society.*

The area around the Sparta compound was quiet during the six-day work cycle. Things got busy on the weekends, however, with Sunday-afternoon soccer games a particular draw for local civilians. "[T]ownspeople would come and stand outside the stockade watching them, even though they weren't supposed to," George Loewe recalled of the spectacle. Children rode their bikes right up to the fence, and according to Hearch Sheckler,

> *It was a real circus with all the people driving by to see the camp. The prisoners were real friendly and would wave to the people. And in the evening, they would build a big campfire and all sit around it and sing German songs. I remember there was one tenor whose voice would take over and tear your heart out.*

Most poignant among the stories about the Peach Ridge POWs is one involving the Lameroux family, whose house stood opposite the camp. People in Sparta agonized as the three blue stars in its front window—through which Alice Lameroux could see the prisoners getting on and off the trucks that took them to work—turned gold, one after the other, marking the combat deaths of sons Al, Donald, and Howard, all in their early twenties. "It was something we didn't want to think about but couldn't help thinking about," a neighbor recalled. "A few of us were worried about what a German war camp, practically in her own back yard, would do to her."

The apprehensions proved unfounded. "My mother was a very strong person," Mrs. Lameroux's daughter explained years later, "and took the camp's presence in stride." Despite her unimaginable grief, at no time did she display even a trace of bitterness or animosity toward the enemy soldiers she watched every day through her window. And the prisoners responded in kind. As they were being dropped off at the gate one afternoon, having heard that yet another "Regret to Inform" telegram had been received at the residence, a detail of men marched across the street in solemn, orderly ranks, stopping at attention just below the porch. There they offered a long, silent salute, executed an about-face and returned, wordlessly, to their compound.

"We've got mothers, too, who lost boys, two, three maybe," Detshel replied when Merlin Kraft asked him why they did it. "We respect everybody who—how you say—*make sacrifice.*"

PART III

WORK

BABY FOOD AND BIRCH TREES

Articles 27 through 34 of the Geneva Convention Relative to the Treatment of Prisoners of War allowed captive enemy combatants to work, under certain conditions. Officers could be assigned to supervisory functions but were otherwise exempt from labor. Enlisted men could volunteer for jobs so long as they were "not directly related to the war effort"—a formulation broadly interpreted in practice, barring prisoners from munitions plants, for example, but permitting them to be employed at all manner of other tasks.

Prisoners in the United States did most of the work preparing their camps for occupancy. Advance teams were brought in to clear brush, erect guard towers and perimeter fences, patch roofs, replace windows and excavate draining ditches. They cleared debris from long-neglected barracks or set up heavy canvas army tents. Once the camps were up and running, POWs assumed clerical, operational and maintenance chores for the entire camp, including those relating to guards and administrators: unloading supply trucks, sweating over laundry, collecting garbage, repairing engines and machinery and working at every stage of mess duty, from baking bread and peeling potatoes to serving tables, scrubbing floors and washing dishes.

Outside of camp, they labored in gangs, not unlike those of the WPA and CCC in the 1930s. They worked in gangs, shoveling asphalt and gravel onto roadbeds. They planted trees, dredged rivers, laid sandbags for flood control, repaired aging bridges and dams, staffed fisheries and tended to recreation facilities in every part of the state.

Prisoners staffed camp supply rooms and laundries. *Courtesy of the Historical Society of Battle Creek.*

Q. M. C. Form No. 365-a
WAR DEPARTMENT
Approved Sept. 5, 1942

QUARTERMASTER LAUNDRY

MONTHLY ROSTER AND STATEMENT
(Extra Sheet)

For month of Sept, 6 1944. , 19

Organization 1631 su P.W. Branch Camp. Station Sparta, Mich.

Name	Laundry Mark	Number of Pieces in Weekly Bundle					Amount due	Charges entered on *
		First Week	Second Week	Third Week	Fourth Week	Fifth Week		
Brainard, Wesley R	B 9234	yes	yes					
Fanning, Geo.	F 9081	yes	yes					
Harwan, John.	H 3041	yes						
Kelly, Jerome A	K 2265	yes	yes					
Loewe, Geo W	L 1175	yes						
Maroney, Thos	M 2278	yes	yes					
Mosciski, Edward	M 6482	yes	yes					
Muir, Frederick	M 4314	yes	yes					
Plaia, Anthony Jr.	P 2759	yes	yes					
Rooklin, Eli	R 6093	yes	yes					
Smith, Morton	S 9064	yes	yes					
Smolinski, Theo	S 9126	yes	yes					
Speth, Harry	S 0579	yes	yes					
Strack, Robert	S 3759	yes	yes					
Tande, Ernest G	T 2820	yes	—					
Taylor, A A	T 6373	yes	yes					
Wright, Seibert M	W 3218	yes	—					
CHAILLAND, Lloyd C	C 0757		yes					
DOMELLE, Adam A	D 5106		yes					
KIRVEN, W. L.	K 8163		yes					
RYAN, P. E.	R 6786		yes					

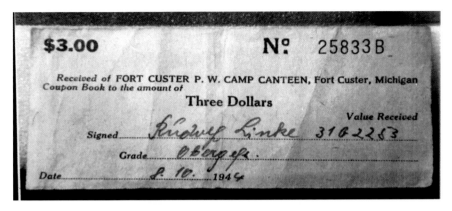

Fort Custer canteen check. *Courtesy of MMTHS.*

The men who did these jobs were entitled to safe conditions and limited hours—no more than ten daily in a six-day week, including transit to and from the work site and a break for lunch.

When they were contracted out to private individuals and businesses, the Geneva Convention directed that POWs be compensated at a level equivalent to the rate for privates in the army. Employers, often with the help of loans from local banks, paid the U.S. Treasury the "prevailing wage" for services rendered, and out of that, prisoners received up to eighty cents a day (beyond a ten-cent basic allowance) in the form of coupons or scrip redeemable at the camp canteen. The remaining balance was substantial, even after deducting maintenance and administrative expenses—easily enough for the system to be self-supporting and even profitable.

The off-site jobs performed in Michigan reflected the state's rich economic diversity. POWs worked in dairy operations near Lansing and on sugar beet and navy bean farms in the Thumb and celery fields near Kalamazoo. They weeded, watered and pulled onions and carrots at Camp Waterloo near Jackson. They painted barns and tended to wheat, corn, mint and tomatoes on the southern border with Ohio. They packed and loaded produce onto refrigeration trucks for the House of David sect in Benton Harbor and cut down trees in the densely wooded wilderness of the Upper Peninsula. And, as we have seen with the case of Emily Foster's family, they climbed ladders in orchards and vineyards all along Lake Michigan, from Oceana, Mecosta and Newaygo Counties down to the Indiana line. They mowed and baled hay, provided manpower for seed and fertilizer plants and kept the lines moving at Heinz, Welch's and other food processing and canning concerns—around the clock at harvest time.

Camp Waterloo, near Jackson. *Courtesy of the Historical Society of Battle Creek.*

Accommodations were of course made for prisoners still nursing battlefield wounds or otherwise bodily impaired. "If a man has a sore back or leg that isn't fully recovered, he is assigned to work he can do without causing further injury," Fort Custer's Major Richter assured the *Battle Creek Enquirer and News.* "Naturally, a perfectly healthy man does a man's job." In any case, the intent was not punitive. To the contrary, in the commandant's experience, the vast majority of POWs "seem to enjoy physical exertion rather than a life of idleness."

By comparing the life cycles of two camps—one near Fremont, northwest of Grand Rapids, the other near the village of Sidnaw in the Upper Peninsula—we can get a sense of the patterns that unfolded in different circumstances and climates all across the state. The former is home to Gerber, founded in 1927 by descendants of German immigrants. Fremont's chamber of commerce boasted of its status as the "Baby Food Capital of the World," and its imposing brick headquarters was a source of pride as an area landmark. Residents were long accustomed to the scent of mashed prunes, pureed squash and steamed spinach that saturated the air for miles around.

By the third year of the war, Fremont faced the same labor crisis confronting so many other small towns and rural communities in Michigan, to one degree or another. Demand for servicemen, enlisted and drafted, threatened steep cuts in production, Gerber's president warned, undermining the war effort and causing perhaps permanent damage to the local economy.

In March 1944, the city council acted to meet the emergency by submitting a request for POW help to the War Manpower Commission branch office in Muskegon. "The plan of using war prisoners in agricultural and canning operations was tried out experimentally in the southern part of the state," explained a city official, citing the success of the pilot camps in Benton Harbor and Caro that had created fierce competition for the limited number of men available. In the spirit of civic responsibility, the unions representing Gerber employees signed on to the idea, after assurances that prisoners would be brought in on a temporary basis only and not present "postwar complications" for returning veterans in search of jobs.

Fremont's critical need was promptly certified. On May 16, an advance team of 25 Germans (guarded by 12 MPs) arrived by truck and got to work setting up accommodations for a larger contingent, stringing barbed wire, digging latrines and the like. "Row after row of neatly-aligned tents first met the eye as one approached the camp behind Gerber's plant," a reporter for the *Fremont Tribune* told his readers. The spacing was designed to allow for clear sight lines from the guard towers. At the end of the month, 274 prisoners were on the grounds, and with the onset of the harvest in late summer, the number swelled to more than 500.

The POWs more than fulfilled their mission, saving the day for the baby-food company, merchants in town and farmers scattered throughout Newago County. By one estimate, they were responsible for eighty-eight thousand man-hours of labor in the first two months of operation alone, with virtually no reported discipline issues. Fremont was another success story, and in October, it was designated as one of only a handful of year-round camps in the state. The prisoners now went to work building the cement block structures that would be their winter quarters.

Amid maple, birch and pine forests in an area "once a hunting ground for the Ojibway," according to the 1940 *WPA Guide to Michigan*, the POW program in the UP included camps near Sidnaw, Rico and Pori in Houghton County and Evelyn and Lake Au Train in Alger County. At their peak, they housed one thousand men, brought in to cut and process trees for Munising Paper, Bonifas Lumber and other area companies.

The resources harvested were of strategic importance, and an argument could be made that the use of prisoners in logging and milling operations in Michigan skirted, if not violated, the Geneva Convention ban on "war-

Historical plaque for Camp Pori in the remote logging country of the western U.P. *Photo by the author.*

related work." Pulpwood was needed to make crates for food, ammunition and tank and plane parts shipped to battle zones across the globe, observed John Pepin of the *Marquette Mining Journal.* It was also used in highway and building construction and in the manufacture of chemicals and explosives. Some of it no doubt found its way into the mountains of bureaucratic memoranda flowing through the new Pentagon in Washington. And some surely went into the psychological warfare payloads being dropped on the cities and towns the prisoners called home. Rick Atkinson noted that in the last year of the war, "Nine million Allied propaganda leaflets fluttered over Germany every day, one thousand tons of paper each month, six billion sheets by war's end, all urging insurrection or surrender."

Camp Sidnaw, off M-28 west of Ishpeming, was established to accommodate a population of 250 POWs. The first of these arrived from Fort Sheridan, Illinois, in February 1944, flashing smiles and waving as they tossed candy to the natives who turned out to see them. The deep freeze into which they were being deposited did not seem to faze them. To the contrary, Jacob Pieti wrote that "[f]or the Germans coming from the deserts of Africa the cold, snowy upper peninsula seemed much more like home."

Guard towers were the only major upgrade required to ready Sidnaw's old CCC camp for its new guests. Fences were deemed unnecessary in such a remote area—the kind of adaptation to local conditions that was commonplace in the POW system across the state. Sentries on patrol with tommy guns and German shepherds were more than sufficient to deter any ideas about breaching the perimeter. Thanks to the camp's intimate size, relations between internees and camp personnel were on the whole friendly and informal.

Tar-paper insulation wrapped the exterior walls of the buildings, crowned with roofs of cedar or shingle. Inside each barracks were thirty cots (as

Sidnaw train depot, 2016. *Photo by the author.*

the camp expanded, double-deck bunks would be installed). Coarse army blankets and woodstoves at each end fended off the bitter nighttime wind. On inspection visits, International Red Cross teams gave Sidnaw consistently high marks ("very clean" and "well-outfitted"), citing the electric lights, the system of water pumps and the quality of the kitchen and infirmary. The latter served civilians in the area as well as camp residents. The soccer field received a lot of use from the prisoners, regardless of the weather, and the rec room had a ping-pong table and other simple amenities.

Problems arose on the job sites, however. Working in three-man teams, the prisoners required a break-in period before they they could operate with any efficiency, and the costs of replacing broken tools, dulled saws and punctured truck tires kept employers in the red for a time. Sabotage was sometimes involved, but inexperience was really the main problem. "[E]ven those who were trying to work hard did a lot of damage," according to Pieti.

Things improved due largely to the initiative and self-policing of the prisoners themselves. "[T]hey soon realized they were going to have to cut the required number of logs a day regardless of the condition of their

Camp Sidnaw barracks and guard tower. *Courtesy of the Houghton County Historical Society.*

equipment, [and] soon took pride in their work and looked down on their fellow POWs who would stir up trouble or [cause] damage," wrote Pieti.

> *They…would often fulfill their quota by ten in the morning and would spend the rest of the day around fires, singing and smoking. Another reason for their change of attitude can be attributed to being forced to walk twelve miles back to camp* [in a snowstorm] *after a particularly unproductive day.*

The people of the Upper Peninsula—descendants of Swedes, Finns, Italians, French Canadians and, to be sure, Native Americans of various tribes—were accustomed to helping one another as a matter of survival in its unforgiving climate, and their approach to these new neighbors was guided by the same spirit.

Civilians offered prisoners advice as they worked beside them in the trees and in the mills. They made small talk—give-and-take about families, mostly, conveyed through the simplest words and gestures—on lunch breaks, or when they encountered them marching in loose formation along gravel logging roads. Pepin described a farmer who threw fresh vegetables into their transport trucks as they passed by, as well as the man who shared his carefully crafted fishing lures with an internee he had befriended on the job. On Sundays, residents turned out to hear their band concerts or watch inter-camp football games, played in the exotic European style. And they offered encouragement to the POWs on their rare excursions into town.

James Goodel's memory of a youthful lapse in etiquette is revealing of the atmosphere in those days. After shouting, "You dirty Nazis!" to a group of Germans he saw walking in downtown Marquette, he recalled being "quickly reminded, with a kick in the rear from his uncle, that he must show them respect." The blow still hurt, even decades later.

There *were* fanatical Hitlerites at Sidnaw and the other camps of the far north, identifiable by their loud voices and defiant, swaggering manner, and they were heckled and shunned with impunity. Pepin records the time "some kids were chased away from a lumber job after they taunted and infuriated the SS soldiers, telling them Germany was losing the war." Word about the incident got around, but none of the boys responsible endured kicks in the rear or any other punishment for their mischief.

More common were experiences like those of Houghton County resident Glen Maki, who recalled with fondness the adventure of skidding logs cut by Sidnaw prisoners. The woods were filled with Germans, Maki recalled, but there was no reason for a youngster like him to be afraid. "It seemed they went out of their way to be nice to me. I think I reminded them of their kid brother they had back home." In a similar vein, Pepin recounted the story of a logger whose wife was known to be expecting their first child: "When the baby was born, several of the POWs asked [him] about the mother's condition. Some had tears in their eyes, reminded of their own wives who had been pregnant when they left for war."

THE BLISSFIELD 16

Despite safeguards and due diligence, the element of risk on the job could never be completely eliminated. Men got hurt thanks to insufficient training, malfunctions in machinery and the inevitable element of human carelessness.

Hazards varied with the circumstances. Harvesting lumber in the U.P. was a notoriously dangerous enterprise, even though, as Pieti noted of Sidnaw, POWs were assigned to stands of smaller, more manageable trees and held to lower quotas than those expected of more experienced loggers and millworkers. Kevin Hall cited the recollections of one Au Train guard:

> We were in the swamps, the worst darn place to cut pulpwood. It was cold, and sometimes we would have two [or] three foot of snow...and those guys are out there trying [to] cut the trees down. They had a lot of accidents, a lot of injuries.

Besides unforgiving blades, falling timber, splinters, choking dust, poison ivy, venomous snakes and frostbite, there were other things to worry about in the north woods wilderness. Sidnaw prisoners wore red armbands on the job and were encouraged "to sing in German or make a lot of noise or something, because we did not want any hunters bearing down on those guys." Music helped pass the time and, so the men were told, ward off the animals whose nocturnal howls made the blood run cold. "Adino and I used to sing *arias* by Verdi or Puccini," a source of friction with some of the Germans, Smolens's Captain Verdi recalls in *Wolf's Mouth*.

And as we have seen, there was yet another danger facing prisoners exiled to the U.P.: the blasts of grenades and machine guns guards used to kill deer.

Work-related accidents were a regular occurrence in the Lower Peninsula as well, most of them mundane or even comic in nature. As a detail of Germans was being transported to the Teichman orchards in Berrien County one morning, they were startled by a sharp *thump* from the front of the truck. No one was hurt, fortunately—no humans, at least. When they returned to their barracks that evening, a prisoner who liked to draw recreated the scene as driver, guard and prisoners stood puzzling over a deceased chicken lying in the middle of the road. The sketch survives, complete with a wry caption that translates to "Another way of hunting."

POWs were entitled to the same care as U.S. soldiers, and a medic—American, German or Italian—accompanied them on the more hazardous work assignments to provide first aid if needed. Back at camp, there was some kind of ambulance on hand, ready to take anyone requiring treatment beyond what was available from the infirmary to the nearest

"Another Way of Hunting." Drawing by a prisoner assigned to the Teichman farm in southwest Michigan. *Courtesy of Bob Myers, Berrien County Historical Society.*

civilian hospital or a larger military facility. There were fatalities—like Otto Scheck, a Custer internee knocked off a truck by a falling wire—but they were rare.

The glaring exception in Michigan was the catastrophe that befell a group of POWs on the commute back to their tent compound on October 31, 1944.

"Blissfield was not the most popular Outside-camp from Fort Custer," recalled Konrad Kreiten in a letter written forty years after the end of the war. The men sent there during harvest season spent long days on acreage throughout Lenawee County pulling and topping beets, an especially labor-intensive task.

> *Long trips in half open trucks to the farmers....We had to finish ½ acre of beets per shift. It could be done in 5-6-7 and sometimes in more than 10 hours. When the ground was loamy and tough, wed [sic] and sticky ectr, it is longer and it takes hard work. We liked better the sandy acres and dry fields! Hands and shoulders became very painful with this unused job. But the guards and farmers had been mostly correct and never drifted or scolded us.*

The morning sky that Wednesday was "low and dark," Kreitan remembered, and it stayed like that all day—in retrospect, perhaps an omen of the trouble to come. At 4:30 p.m., a ton-and-a-half army truck carrying twenty-four prisoners back to camp from the Raymond Beck farm approached a rail crossing on the rough gravel of Silberhorn Road, half a mile east of Blissfield. The men were tired but in good spirits, looking forward to the Halloween festivities planned for that evening. As their truck proceeded across the tracks, a westbound New York Central passenger train slammed into it, full force, just behind the cab.

The vehicle was dragged forty feet along the right-of-way, according to the headline story in the *Blissfield Advance* the next day. Men were sent flying upward of 300 feet from the point of impact. "[T]he bodies of three of the Pws were caught on the pilot of the engine and carried about 1,800 feet down the tracks," the *Advance* told its readers, past Ireland's Alfalfa Mill. Sixteen prisoners were killed, most of them instantly, along with twenty-year-old Edward B. Loughrin, their American guard.

It was past midnight before the last of the dead had been recovered and identified. Emergency crews rushed the injured to general hospitals in Adrian and Toledo, among them Pascual Martinez, the forty-two-year-old

Blissfield Advance, November 1, 1945. *Courtesy of Blissfield Public Library.*

driver, who was unconscious from the collision. Martinez, who had a good safety record, later told police he never saw the train coming. An army board of inquiry later cleared him from blame, noting the trees and tall weeds obstructing the view at the crossing.

The calamity made national news alongside the latest reports from overseas battlefields. People from surrounding communities, especially the farmers and their families who had gotten to know the prisoners on a personal level, shared in the shock and anguish that engulfed everyone in the camp as the dimensions of the tragedy sank in. The Halloween party was, needless to say, canceled, the homemade masks and costumes left unworn, the special meal prepared for the occasion largely uneaten. Kreitan would never forget the vacant expressions he saw among his friends in the tent city that night. "It was quite [*sic*], quite as dead," he wrote. Still, the routines of the harvest made their demands, and the next day, "the work went on, what else could we do."

Loughrin's body was sent to his family in Cadillac for burial. The others who perished were interred on Saturday, November 3, in a section of Custer's cemetery set aside for POWs. There were three services conducted

This page and opposite: Funeral services and burial for the Blissfield 16 on November 3, 1945. *Courtesy of the Historical Society of Battle Creek.*

Funeral services and burial for the Blissfield 16 on November 3, 1945. *Courtesy of the Historical Society of Battle Creek.*

that day, the *Advance* reported—one Lutheran, one a Holy Mass for the seven Catholics and one for the men who were listed as "non-religious." The coffins were adorned with German flags rushed by air from the army quartermaster in Philadelphia.

The next day, Camp Blissfield, by order of its commander, Captain Richard Bemont, held its own rites for the victims. In attendance were the Reverend C.H. Schmelzer of Riga and Father Leo Thiesen of St. Peter's Catholic Church, clergy who held weekly services in German at the compound. With the aid of a translator, the Revered H.C. Brubaker gave the homily from a specially constructed platform, looking out onto row upon row of POWs who had taken seats on the ground. At its front was a plaque listing the names of the dead.

> *Philip Allmann*
> *Franz Allmer*
> *Ferdinand Auer*
> *August Baumgartner*
> *Hans Becker*
> *Norbert Berhhofer*
> *Anton Beckmann*
> *Karl Acker*
> *Richard Ackermann*
> *Ernst Ahrens*
> *Rolf Arnold*
> *Kurt Bernock*
> *Karl Arzberger*
> *Heinz Bialetzki*
> *Kurt Behring*
> *Paul Beiersdörfer*

The camp orchestra provided musical accompaniment, and hymns filled the autumn air. A violin solo of "Ave Maria"—"beautifully played by one of the prisoners," according the *Advance* correspondent who covered the event—brought tears to the eyes of administrators, staff and MPs who listened, united in grief with their charges. The ceremony closed with full military protocol:

> *The prisoners were* [summoned] *to order by* [their] *company commander, and as they stood at attention he read the roll of honor, while the orchestra*

played Ich hatt einen Kameraden, *the German bugler sounded taps and three volleys were fired by an eight-man firing squad.*

At 2:15 p.m., in a final gesture of tribute, the machinery at the nearby Great Lakes Sugar Company ground to a halt, allowing regular employees and POW workers to pause together for one minute of silent reflection.

ESCAPE?

Thanks to the generally favorable treatment given prisoners shipped to America, as well as the manifest unlikelihood of success, escape attempts were strikingly small in number. Marooned in a remote and unfamiliar landscape, their grasp of English limited at best, the big letters PW stenciled all over their work fatigues—for most, the logic of flight just didn't add up. "It's not the guards or the snow fence that keeps us in," went the camp saying, "it's the Atlantic Ocean." A Custer official told the *Detroit Times* that in his experience "only a 'few dumbells' have the slightest thought of trying to run away." The Germans working on the Teichman farm in Berrien County understood the situation. When I inquired about the light security under which they operated, Emily Foster assured me, with a knowing smile, that "they weren't *going* anywhere."

Despite the long odds, a few did aspire to freedom, however hazy the path to that goal might be. For some, bound by the soldier's duty to at least *try* to escape, the effort involved elaborate coordination and planning. A repurposed mining tunnel extending 150 feet, the result of countless hours of clandestine activity, was discovered before it could be used at Camp Trinidad in Colorado. Prisoners at Fort Ord in California dug a similar subterranean passageway 120 feet in length.

Others acted more impulsively, driven by fear, restlessness or just a desperate longing to reunite with their families somehow. For them, evening darkness or the daytime hours spent outside camp, in transit to or from the job site or during rest breaks, offered the most tempting opportunities for action. Perhaps they would make the move when the blinding beam of the searchlight traced away from their sector of the compound or when the guard took his regular afternoon nap. Once out, the hope was that there would be friendly civilians to offer food and at least temporary shelter.

This happens for John Smolens's protagonist in *Wolf's Mouth*. Under a sentence of death from the camp Nazis, Giuseppe Verdi and the Russian loner who shares his work detail drop their axes one day and walk off into the hills surrounding Lake Au Train. As they go their separate ways and the racket of voices and saw blades recedes into the winter silence, Verdi is suddenly struck with a sense of isolation and dread. "After only a few steps I realized that I had no choice," he remembers later. "[I]t was impossible for me to go back."

Through pine forests and across logging roads, Verdi makes his way to the harbor town of Munising, to the home of a young Italian American woman he had connected with on brief trips outside camp. Chiara and her mother are from a community of *immigranti* who had arrived in the Upper Peninsula to labor in its now-depleted copper and iron ore quarries and mines. They agree to hide him as he considers his options.

Verdi settles on Detroit as the next stop—five hundred miles distant, according to the map. Given the risks involved, it might as well be the moon. To get there, he has to travel east to catch the ferry that crosses the Straits of Mackinac at St. Ignace or west on a circuitous journey by way of Wisconsin and Chicago. He chooses the Michigan route for what he realizes even then are "irrational reasons": the state "was peninsulas, two of them, and there were villages named after saints," reminding him of home. Through sleet, snow and brushes with the law, Giuseppe and Chiara manage to get their borrowed car to the Motor City, where, with help, they establish new identities.

This kind of adventure hardly ever happened in real life. War Department records show that of the more than 400,000 POWs interned across the United States, fewer than 1 percent tried to escape. Most of those who did were apprehended within twenty-four hours.

There were exceptions in the Michigan system. A pair of Dundee prisoners rode a freight boxcar all the way to Roanoke, Virginia—en route, they imagined, to Mexico—before authorities tracked them down. In the late summer of 1944, Franz Janoszek, a twenty-nine-year-old internee at the Hartford sub-camp, remained at large for four days after making a break for it while on the job at an orchard near Eau Claire. Following his recapture, Janoszek was transferred to Fort Custer, where a second attempt a month later ended in self-inflicted tragedy. State police discovered his body—run over by a Grand Trunk train—on a track at the southeastern boundary of the camp grounds. The engineer said that by the time he saw the man step out from the tall grass and place himself in harm's way, it was too late to stop.

This irreversible method of escape was newsworthy but not unique. The publicity surrounding it brought pressure on administrators to better manage the morale of those under their watch. "The army was worried recently by what it thought was a wave of prisoner suicides," the *Battle Creek Enquirer and News* reported in the wake of the Janoszek incident. An actuarial study quashed alarms about an epidemic, however, finding the rate in the average POW camp lower than that of civilians living in cities of comparable population.

Michigan's scattered incidents of escape fit the national pattern of futility. In July 1944, the Fremont commander put out an alert for Johann Schumacher, Wilhelm Winetzke and Kurt Lison—three prisoners working at Gerber who failed to answer the evening roll call. Police found the trio within hours, fast asleep in a barn loft near Hart, just north of camp. A phone tip about a suspicious character seen walking along a Newago County road led authorities to Fritz Schwindt, another Fremont internee, as he hid under packing crates in the local pea-processing plant. Tired, hungry and directionless, Waterloo escapee Heinz Eschweiler surrendered himself in similarly short order, having made it only three miles from camp.

First-time offenders received the same discipline that applied to an American soldier gone AWOL—digging ditches and extra mess chores, along with a forfeiture of privileges like access to the rec room. More serious cases brought guardhouse confinement with a diet of bread and water or transfer to Custer or another base camp. To its credit, the United States was one of the few combatant nations to exclude the gallows or the firing squad as options for such infractions.

Camp Lakewood, a converted CCC camp at a bend in the Kalamazoo River, housed 650 mostly German POWs its nineteen months of operation (May 21, 1944–January 4, 1946). Arriving in groups of 200 or 250, they were assigned to agricultural jobs throughout the southwestern corner of Michigan. They weeded and harvested onions, carrots, beans, potatoes, corn and mint on farms near Fennville and Hopkins. In orchards around Bangor, South Haven and Saugatuck, they gathered bushels of cherries, peaches, plums and apples. And according to Ken Kuipers of the *Holland Sentinel*, they supplemented the workforce at the H.J. Heinz pickling plant, Weller Nurseries, Lake Shore Sugar, the Allegan Muck Growers Association, Michigan Fruit Canners, Welch's Grape in Mattawan, Pet Milk in Wayland and the South Haven Chemical Company. During the winter, they could be seen shoveling snow and salting roads for the Holland Board of Public Works.

Lakewood prisoners developed the usual rapport with both the landscape and its inhabitants. "It looked a lot like Europe," remembered Gerd Lindemann, the Afrika Corps officer charged with work assignments and discipline at the camp. The desk job bored him, so he waived his exemption and joined his men in the fields. "I wanted to meet the people," Lindemann later explained. "We became acquainted to farms, and the farmers treated us right." He saw in their fairness and decency the best in the national character. "The people here, it's an American tradition: They feel for the underdog."

The good opinion was mutual. The prisoners gave a good day's work to their employers and easily won their respect. "We couldn't converse with them, but they whistled," recalled area grower Robert Crane of the ride to and from the orchards. "These guys, if they didn't have POW painted on their backs, looked like your neighbors." Crane mocked those in his community who had so loudly voiced their concerns about security. "Gee," he told a reporter, "do you think they're gonna escape with my little Ford tractor and steal a load of peaches?"

The record was not perfect, however. Camp Lakewood recorded six escape attempts, all of them short-lived affairs. Twenty-two-year-old George Lunz made the front page of the *County News* when he disappeared into the woods as his mates took their weekly Sunday swim in Lake Allegan. Hastily mustered search parties spent a long night looking for him in Swan Creek Marsh, a place known for its "man-eating" mosquitoes.

Eager to give himself up the next morning, Lunz presented himself at the farmhouse door of Mr. and Mrs. William Wall. The couple spoke German to their surprise guest as they invited him in for a full course of country hospitality—bath and breakfast, ointment for his cuts, scratches and bites, even a leisurely nap—before driving him to the police station in downtown Allegan. "The searchers, most of whom were were subjected to the same briars and 'skeeters' during the 24-hour chase, didn't exactly greet the Walls with open arms after hearing that [he] had been with them most of the day," reported the *Kalamazoo Gazette*.

Once in custody, Lunz explained the motivation behind his flight: a new Lakewood prisoner informed him that his brother was being held in another

POW camp, so he set out, on foot, to join him there. Lunz was sent to Fort Custer, but it was clear to the officials who talked to him that this was a case of naiveté rather than incorrigible rebellion. Soon enough, Lunz was granted his wish: transfer to finish out the war with his brother—in St. Louis.

Josef Mets betrayed a similarly unrealistic grasp of scale and geography when he slipped out of Camp Lakewood at 3:00 a.m. one Sunday morning. He was picked up the next day, tramping along the shoulder of a county road fifteen miles south of Allegan. A Yugoslav who had volunteered for Hitler's Wehrmacht, Mets told MPs of his (justifiable) fear of being condemned as a traitor when he was eventually sent home. What was the destination of refuge he had chosen? Where was he headed? "South America," came the earnest reply.

From his office in Washington, J. Edgar Hoover warned that every POW at large represented "a danger to our internal security, our war production, and the lives and safety of our citizens." This was alarmist, but for law enforcement, from the FBI on down, the task of pursuing escapees was no joke, at least until they were safely apprehended. Sheriff Louis Johnson took no chances when he organized a posse of deputies to locate four Lakewood fugitives. Word of a group of young men obviously not from the area, "dressed in raincoats with bundles over the shoulders," led to the suspects walking in the morning fog along M-40. When Sheriff Johnson barked out a "Halt!" order, three of them surrendered immediately, according to the *Allegan County News*, "but it took a second command and a show of weapons for the fourth to raise his hands aloft." Not every prisoner was cooperative, and a wary caution in these cases was understandable.

"CONSPIRACY" IN OWOSSO

I t's easy to imagine how POWs reacted when they encountered the opposite sex, however briefly or indirectly. Though otherwise applauded for their correct manners, these young men did not hesitate to offer invitations and whistles to the young females they saw through the barbed wire or on their daily commutes to work.

The attraction seemed to be mutual. A Detroit woman in her eighties laughed when she told me how she and her friends used to walk to the state fairgrounds (where some Italians were held) or take the bus down to Fort Wayne to ogle and flirt—adventures wisely kept from their parents. Another recalled waving at Italian men dancing with one another, a sight hilarious to the teenaged imagination. No doubt, curious youngsters throughout Michigan were engaged in like activities, smuggling letters, tossing candy bars and cookies over the fence and developing "romances" with their favorites—who, of course, promised to marry them, once the war was over.

The Italians' status changed once their country quit the war in September 1943. Those who volunteered (upward of 90 percent, according to Camilla Calamandrei) became members of Italian Service Units (ISUs). The men at Fort Wayne did manual and clerical jobs at army posts and airfields like Selfridge and Romulus. They worked as orderlies in military hospitals and stevedores in the warehouses of the U.S. Quartermaster Corps. ISU members were permitted a freedom of movement outside camp unavailable to POWs, which sometimes might include sightseeing

Italian Service Unit (ISU)
volunteers at Detroit's Fort
Wayne. *Courtesy of Reuther Archives.*

excursions around the city or even a much-coveted weekend pass (*la libera
uscita*) enforced on the honor system.

And a large Italian American community stood ready to embrace them.
"In Detroit alone, they support three newspapers and 101 musical, fraternal,
literary and political societies," noted the 1940 *WPA Guide to Michigan.*
Catholic parishes hosted picnics and dances and holiday celebrations for
ISU members, carefully chaperoned along the lines of USO mixers for off-
duty American troops. Families were encouraged to invite them to their

homes for Sunday meals—elaborate multicourse feasts, topped off with grandmother's cannoli.

Interaction with the opposite sex on these occasions, however innocent, did not meet with everyone's approval, especially among those who had loved ones in the line of fire overseas. And rumors about "what the girls back home were doing" made many a GI's blood boil, as evidenced in letters to *Stars and Stripes* and other publications. But the interactions continued, through the end of the war and beyond.

Catherine Previdi never forgot the day a chance encounter with an Italian Service Unit man changed her life. She tells her story in Louis Keefer's *Italian Prisoners of War in America*:

> *While the ISU men were here in Detroit, serving at Fort Wayne, a lot of… families welcomed them to their homes for a visit or a dinner. That's how I met and fell in love with Romano. A friend asked me over to talk with the fellows and then we all danced on the kitchen floor to music played on the Victrola. That was November 11, 1944. From then on it was always Romano and Catherine.*

> *All the company would get together and pool their money and rent a hall and have dances as often as three nights a week. The girls paid 25-cents admission to help with the cost of the music and drinks. It was soda pop only, nothing hard. Romano and I never jitterbugged. Just the old fox trots, waltzes and slow-dancing, holding one another. None of this modern stuff of dancing apart. We had such good times.*

The fact that she was never "officially" engaged to Romano did not present a problem. "It was just sort of understood that we would get married when the war was over," recalled Previdi. "There wasn't even any worrying about how I would get over there or how we two would get back."

The workplace was another zone of co-ed fraternization, and indeed the temptations arising from long hours in proximity on the job were at the root of the single most sensational scandal of Michigan's wartime POW program. The facts were these: At about 5:30 p.m. on Thursday, July 20, 1944, a Ford sedan carrying two women from the Shiawassa County village of Bennington—Kitty Case, twenty, and Shirley Druce, nineteen—proceeded to a prearranged location behind the W.W. Roach Cannery building in Owosso, where they had been discharged earlier in the week.

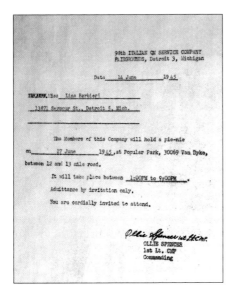

Official notice of a "pic-nic" in suburban Detroit, organized for the Fort Wayne Italians. *Courtesy of Reuther Archives.*

Gottfried Hobel and Erik Classen, twenty-year-old Germans from the speedway prison camp west of town, emerged on cue from the brush and climbed into the back seat of the car. For Afrika Corps commandos, this kind of mission was child's play.

Behind the wheel was Phyllis Case, Kitty's seventeen-year-old half sister. "I had better drive where she told me to or get my head knocked off," Phyllis later recalled of the threats from the passenger seat as she drove the foursome around for the next several hours. According to her courtroom testimony, as the daylight faded, the younger girl used the excuse of a gas gauge headed toward empty to extricate herself from the situation, dropping the others off, as directed, at Colby Lake near Corunna in Woodhull Township.

Phyllis rushed home to tell her stepmother, Alberta Case, why she had been out so late, and they drove together to the speedway to sound the alert, arriving there about 10:30 p.m. Kitty had a history of "undisciplined and headstrong" behavior, Mrs. Case would tell police, and had announced her plans to run away from home that very afternoon—so the fact that she was in so much trouble came as no surprise.

The barracks were dark and the prisoners were asleep in their bunks, but the absence of Hobel and Classen, to the camp commander's considerable embarrassment, had yet to be noticed. A manhunt ensued, led by the sheriff's departments of Shiawasee and Ingham Counties and the Michigan State Police. The fugitives were found and apprehended in a patch of woods near Colby Lake the next morning about 7:00 a.m.

"War Prisoners Aided by Girls, Flee, Caught," read the headline of Friday afternoon's *Owosso Argus-Press.* "The group was in a jovial, laughing mood at the moment of their capture," the paper reported, and not all that forthcoming besides.

Hobel, one of the prisoners, speaks very fair English and Classen is believed to understand it, but when addressed in English [he] just shrugs his shoulders and says nothing.

In posing for their pictures this morning, the Case girl said she wanted to get as close to Hobel as possible, and asked for a print of the picture.

The prisoners were told of the attempt on the life of Adolph [sic] Hitler reported Thursday. Hobel read it carefully, then, with a scornful wave of the hand, said "Rot," no good.

During the night, according to the girls, they bet among themselves that they would be caught within 24 hours.

Hobel and Classen were turned over to Camp Owosso MPs. After they made another escape attempt a month later, disappearing with two other Germans from a work detail on a Gratiot County farm, the repeat offenders were shipped off to Custer and then transported by train to a more locked-down POW facility in New Mexico.

If Kitty Case and Shirley Druce thought their road trip would be seen as a lark or a misguided search for adventure, as a petty act of spite to get back at the company that had fired them (for drinking on the job) or as a date growing out of a pedestrian workplace romance—in short, something harmless, quickly forgiven and forgotten—they were mistaken. It may have been a combination of all these things, but this was wartime, and the shock waves from what they had done reverberated in ways they never imagined. Photographs of the pair in court, their tear-stained faces shifting in expression from abject sadness to contrition, would sell a lot of newspapers over the coming months, and the details of their story would fuel hometown gossip for the rest of their lives.

Federal authorities debated about how to deal with the accused. The editorial

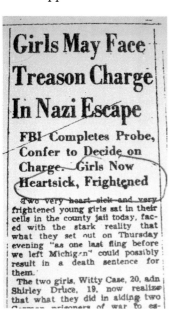

Girls May Face Treason Charge In Nazi Escape

FBI Completes Probe, Confer to Decide on Charge. Girls Now Heartsick, Frightened

Two very heart-sick and very frightened young girls sat in their cells in the county jail today, faced with the stark reality that what they set out on Thursday evening "as one last fling before we left Michigan" could possibly result in a death sentence for them.

The two girls, Witty Case, 20, and Shirley Druce, 19, now realize that what they did in aiding two German prisoners of war to es-

"Two very heart sick and very frightened young girls sat in the county jail today." *Courtesy of Owosso Public Library.*

page of the *Argus-Press* urged the public to be patient with the process, arguing that while American-style due process was slow and sometimes clumsy, it was a thing in which readers should take pride. "If the case was reversed and two German girls had been caught with a couple of prisoners of war, [their] fate would probably not be in doubt." One option was to simply "throw the book at them" with a charge of treason. "Two very heart sick and very frightened young girls sat in their cells in the county jail today," the paper reported in its Saturday edition, "faced with the stark reality that what they set out [to do] on Thursday evening could possibly result in a death sentence for them."

Kitty Case, the more talkative of the two, gave her version of events to FBI agents from Detroit during an all-day "grilling" session:

> *Shirley wanted to go to see her boy friend, who is in the Navy, and I decided to go with her. We thought this would be just one last fling before we left. We thought we would take the prisoners with us as far as our gas lasted, then forget them and hitchhike to Virginia. But what a fling it turned out to be.*

Kitty told the agents she sold a cow Thursday morning, netting more than fifty dollars to finance the scheme. She maintained that the fugitive night was spent awake and just talking—trying to paint the end in the most innocent light:

> *We were standing in the woods looking at some Kodak pictures of boy and girl friends and showing them to the two prisoners. Suddenly Shirley exclaimed: "There's the police!"*
>
> *"This is no time to joke, don't try to kid me," I replied, then looking around and there were the officers. There was nothing for us to do but surrender.*

It was decided that prosecution for treason was too severe a course, given the brevity of the offense and the lack of any real harm done. As one FBI interrogator explained, "[T]he girls indicated they had no sympathy with the Nazi cause," and however foolish, their actions amounted to "just an escapade of juvenile delinquents." After two days in custody, the Justice Department in Washington ordered that Case and Druce be released to their families without charge.

Local reactions to this show of leniency were mixed, if the calls received by the Owosso sheriff's department are any indication. "Some threatened violence to the girls, while others expressed sympathy," the *Argus-Press* reported. "One woman telephoned that she had prayed all night for them." Most felt the girls deserved *some* kind of punishment, if only to make an example of what happened to civilians who got too friendly with POWs— even if, in this case, the men were "for the most part ordinary fellows, who are not particularly dangerous in themselves."

Late Monday night, barely twenty-four hours after the girls' release, two FBI agents, a deputy U.S. marshal and matron and a local police officer were dispatched to rearrest them. The warrants were based on the creatively applied lesser charge of "conspiracy to defraud the government by impairing, obstructing and defeating the lawful function of the War Department in [its] custody of prisoners of war under the provisions of the Geneva Convention." Mrs. George Shaw, Druce's guardian, "was shocked by the unexpected turn of events and sobbed bitterly," the next day's *Argus-Press* observed of the scene.

> *There was some delay while waiting for Shirley to dress, and when she left* [Mrs. Shaw] *became hysterical. Relatives were summoned to care for her. As Shirley walked calmly out of the house, she told the others to "take care of grandma. I'll be back soon."*

Druce and Case were arraigned in federal court in Bay City, then released again, on bail, pending ultimate determination of their fate. In the face of a grand jury indictment, the Owosso attorney retained to represent them held fast to their plea of innocence.

As to be expected, the trial in the deep freeze of January 1945 was a media circus and the subject of passionate debate well beyond Michigan's borders. The testimony presented over its four days, some of it salacious (by the standards of the day), much of it conflicted, brought forth further details of the escape episode and put it within its larger context.

The press ran with the story of Kitty Case as "the American sweetheart" of Gottfried Hobel, the handsome young soldier who promised to return after the war so they could get married. Weeks before the fateful day, according to the records of the Owosso Public Library, Case checked out a German-language dictionary in preparation for their union. She and best friend Shirley hitchhiked into town that Thursday morning, borrowed Alberta Case's car and then spent the afternoon cruising the stores of the business district. Druce insisted that Phyllis Case was not as unwitting an accomplice as she pretended. No coercion was needed to convince her to drive the getaway vehicle, she said, and at one point Phyllis even kissed one of the prisoners and "made [him] sing for her."

The most disturbing theme to emerge at trial was the pattern of negligence and lax security that prevailed at both the cannery work site, with its assigned detail of 345 POWs, and at Camp Owosso itself. "Wholesale drinking" on the job (with guards and foremen supplying the whiskey, beer and wine) happened every day, along with "water battles," softball games and fistfights among the prisoners. "One called the other an S.O.B.," Robert McAvoy recalled. "He answered something about not insulting his mother. And soon they were rolling around on the ground hitting each other."

Then there was the passing of notes, like the one from Hobel to Kitty Case setting up their July 20 rendezvous. The evidence revealed an elaborate underground communication network through which POWs solicited sexual contact and other forms of mischief with their female co-workers, many of them minors. "A lot of the girls thought the prisoners were cute," Case said in her written statement. "Some of us select[ed] one…saying 'He's mine.'" Meanwhile, late-night trysts were common outside the gates of the speedway, right under the noses of the guards.

The U.S. attorney seized upon these disclosures, using them to appeal to the jury's sense of patriotism. "While these girls slept in a field with the enemy," the prosecution declared of the night spent near Colby Lake, "lots of our boys are sleeping their last days in battlefields all over the world."

The picture of gross negligence on the homefront reached soldiers in some of those battlefields. Clarence Hughes, a Marine private slogging his way through beach landings in the Pacific, was so incensed by a *Time* article he read about the trial that he decided to write an open letter to the Owosso Chamber of Commerce, duly published in the *Argus-Press*. The story "has caused considerable comment among the members of our outfit," Private Hughes began, warming to his subject.

> *We should like to take this opportunity to express our complete disapproval and disappointment in the contemptable [sic], inefficient method in which this city's prosecution of law and order is being handled. It is indeed a sad state of affairs, after reading about the constant maltreatment of American war prisoners, to discover that alleged patriots in our midst who, unmindful of the grim tragedy that war really is, nonchalantly ignore the duties of their positions and permit such outrageous conduct to occur.*

It is our firm belief the Army MP detachment at the prisoner-of-war camp, Owosso, Michigan, should immediately be transferred to the European front lines, where they would be privileged to observe some real soldiers in action and would most assuredly be taught the fundamentals of military discipline in a hurry.

Counsel for Case and Druce offered up a smorgasbord of defenses. These included arguments that his clients' statements to the FBI had been coerced and that the tavern owners who sold alcohol to them bore at least partial responsibility for their impaired judgment. He requested dismissal of the case, on the grounds that using prisoners for food production "furthered the war effort" in violation of the Geneva Convention. And he noted, finally, that the girls came from "broken homes," and a fleeting, impetuous "call of youth" caused them to err that day in July. This last was too much for the prosecuting lawyer, who added it to his invocations of duty. "The only call of youth I know today is the call to the colors of the country," he declared when his time came to speak.

After four and a half hours of deliberation, the jury came back with a verdict of guilty. When the foreman read it, the "emotionless" courtroom demeanor of the defendants suddenly cracked, and they collapsed into the arms of their loved ones, "sobbing violently."

The caption of the photograph in the *Bay City Times* showing the convicted pair as they stood before Judge Frank Picard at a final hearing a month later, on February 13, gives us the flavor of the sexism that was then just a matter of routine: "Blonde, buxom Kitty Marie Case…who appeared in court with white bobby socks, black sweater and red skirt, is pictured on the left. Slim Shirley Jean Druce…is wearing a gold dress and brown sports coat."

The defendants "sobbed violently" when the verdict was read. *Courtesy of Owosso Public Library.*

Judge Picard handed down a sentence of one year and three months in federal prison for Case, the apparent mastermind of the conspiracy, and one year and one day for Druce, minus time already served. He took the opportunity to remind them of the far more serious charges they might have faced. "I have taken into consideration that all blame for what happened doesn't rest on your

Owosso Girls Get Terms in Federal Prison

Sent to Prison

Kitty Case to Serve Year, 3 Months. Shirley Druce Year, and Day For Aiding Nazis

Terms in federal prison were imposed this morning on two Owosso girls who admitted helping two German prisoners of war escape from the plant of the W. R. Roach Canning Co. here last July 20. They were sentenced by Judge Frank A. Picard in Federal Court in Bay City.

Kitty Marie Case, 21, drew one year and three months and Shirley Jean Druce, 19, was given one year and a day. The prison where they will serve their time will be designated later by the United States attorney general's department. Judge Picard stated, however, that in view of the fact that they had served one month, they may be considered for parole when one-third of their sentences is served.

After being sentenced in Federal Court, the two girls appeared at hearings held by Commissioner Felix Flynn of the Michigan Liquor Control Commission and gave testimony which resulted in the conviction of two Owosso and one Corunna, liquor licensees, of selling liquor to minors.

Defers Penalties

Commissioner Flynn deferred imposing penalties on them until the entire Liquor Commission can review the testimony. He said he did this because of the serious results of their violations. The li...

KITTY CASE

SHIRLEY DRUCE

Girls Go to Prison fo Aiding Nazis Escap

The self-styled "search for venture" of two Owosso girls v spent a night in the woods 1 summer with Nazi prisoners v fled with them in the hope of jc ing their own army ended today prison sentences.

Kitty Marie Case, 21, was ord ed to serve a year and three mon in jail, while her associate, Shir Marie Druce, 18, was sentenced a year and a day in prison.

Both stood calmly as they he Federal Judge Frank A. Pic pronounce sentence in fede court here for conspiracy to fraud the government by aid Gottfried Hobel and Erit Class former members of General Rc mel's Africa Korps, to escape fr a work detail at the W. R. Ro Canning Co. in Owosso last Jt

Quizzed on Liquor Charges

Immediately after sentence, girls were closeted with repres tatives of the Michigan Liq Control commission for interro tion on charges they made in trial of purchasing intoxicat liquors in Owosso and Corun taverns.

They are the only girls in

SHIRLEY DRUCE   KITTY CASE

Transport Plane Crackup Kills 24

Prison terms for the Owosso "conspirators" changed their lives forever. *Courtesy of Owosso Public Library.*

shoulders," he added in a tone of paternal reassurance. Their folly was aided and abetted by many other careless people, military and civilian alike.

Still, the judge insisted with a scolding stare, they should be mindful that their selfish stunt, seen from the perspective of the war raging beyond the isolation of small-town Michigan, could well have had dire consequences:

> *If these two men you aided had been able to make their way back to Germany, they would have gotten there just in time to participate in last December's Ardennes break-through which cost 100,000 American casualties and in which German soldiers in cold blood shot and killed unarmed Americans who had surrendered.*

Given the pressures of the moment, the criminal justice system handled Kitty Case and Shirley Druce, two youngsters full of post-adolescent boredom, caught in "the wrong place at the wrong time," with an admirable mix of gravity, prudence and compassion. But the trauma of the process, compounded by the sensational press coverage (and the word-of-mouth innuendo it fueled, which continues to this day), left them with scars that would never heal.

After serving out their prison terms, the woman got as far away from Shiawassee County as possible. Kitty moved to Georgia, and Shirley relocated to California; they both married and raised families. For a 2010 retrospective on the scandal, an *Argus-Press* reporter tracked down Melinda Nethaway, Druce's daughter-in-law, who said that the misadventure and the troubles that followed it remained a closely guarded secret for decades, a source of shame Shirley withheld even from her children until her (early) death. "To be honest, I don't think anyone was shocked," Nethaway mused of the belated disclosure. "I think [we all] knew that there was always something in the closet."

Despite the tabloid glare of the Owosso escape "conspiracy," county residents developed a generally warm attitude toward the Germans at the speedway, and the news about them was not all negative. "WAR PRISONERS RESCUE WOMAN AS HOME BURNS," read an *Argus-Press* headline on July 7, 1945, six months after the Case/Druce trial. Half a century later, Eva Worthington, still sharp at eighty-one, was full of gratitude for those who had come to her aid in a life-threatening emergency that summer day.

It was the pea harvest season, and the prisoners were pulling eighteen-hour shifts under her husband Frank's supervision at the Roach Cannery, a block across the railroad tracks from their house on Garfield Avenue in the southeast part of town. Just home from Memorial Hospital after giving birth to her tenth child, Mrs. Worthington was asleep in bed when sparks from a passing freight train set fire to the wood-shingled roof.

Patsy, I believe, was at my side, but I have trouble recalling what happened. I think I was going into shock or slipping away from smoke inhalation. I can remember to this day hearing the crackling noise and feeling the heat, but I just couldn't wake up. The kids couldn't get me out because they were all so young, were scared, and I'm a big woman.

Several of the POWs who were working outside the factory saw the flames and smoke coming from the house. Remember, they were under armed guard, yet dropped their tools and started running toward the house anyway. I think the guards may have seen the fire and, luckily for me, realized what the Germans were trying to do before any shots were fired.

War Prisoners Rescue Woman As Home Burns

Mother and Babe Are Carried Out Of Garfield Avenue Home

The German prisoner of war can be a gentleman—if he wants to, so states Mr. Frank Worthington, of 532 Garfield avenue. Mrs. Worthington arrived home yesterday afternoon from Memorial Hospital where she had been in confinement and was peacefully dozing about 8 o'clock last evening, when she was aroused by a group of people.

"The German prisoner of war can be a gentleman when he wants to be." *Courtesy of Owosso Public Library.*

After scaling a security fence, the prisoners fought their way through heat and smoke into the burning house, wrapped Mrs. Worthington in a mattress and carried her out to safety. Some went back in several times to salvage the family's furnishings and mementoes, while others helped Owosso firemen string hose to fight the blaze. The structure was a total loss, but no one was seriously injured.

"The German prisoner of war can be a gentleman when he wants to be," Eva Worthington told a reporter on the scene at the time. She never did learn who among the men had acted to prevent the tragedy— but she had her suspicions.

I used to take Frank's lunch and dinner over to him at the factory when they were working such long hours. There was this one blonde, very handsome young prisoner who liked to hold Patsy. I'd let him coddle and caress her each time I'd visit the plant. He said he had a wife and daughter back in Germany.

I got a letter from him a while after they'd been returned home. Somehow I misplaced or lost the letter down through the years, but I can recall him thanking me for the decent treatment he and the others received while being held prisoner.

I've always had this feeling that he was one of those who entered the house that night and saved my life. I never heard from him after that one letter.

PART IV

DOING TIME

MAIL CALL, ALCOHOL AND "YANKEE" WAYS

Despite the distractions of work and the relative comfort of their accommodations, homesickness and boredom remained ever-constant adversaries for Michigan's POWs. Theirs was a life, after all, suspended in limbo, in a circumscribed world where days and weeks blurred, seemingly without end. In *Wolf's Mouth*, Verdi describes the restlessness that stalks him at Au Train during his waking hours and in dreams. Even the camp's name has an ironic and mocking quality:

> *Americans call it* doing time, *but I didn't look at it that way. Time moved forward, but I remained stationary—it was the train, and I was standing on the platform unable to board because the locomotive, though it might slow down, never stopped.*

Washington officials and camp administrators alike understood the need to keep their charges busy during their off hours, and the prisoners embraced the recreational opportunities made available to them, adapting them to their own creative ways of "doing time." AP correspondent Kathryn Umphrey explained the thinking behind the latitude they had with regard to leisure. "The lot of any war prisoner, even in this country, is none too good," she concluded after visiting Fort Custer. "It is a long, monotonous round of hard work. Any measures that help create good morale increase the amount of work done and consequently any reasonable diversion prisoners contrive is allowed."

When internees returned from a typical day out on the job, they washed up and then gathered in the camp mess to share—over soldierly complaints and boisterous talk—the evening meal. Once the housekeeping chores in and around the compound were finished, they were considered "at ease," and the hours remaining until lights out (promptly at 10:00 p.m.) were theirs to use as they saw fit. "We know of and are interested in only that portion of the PW day which is between 'count' in the morning and 'count' in the evening," went the rule of thumb among camp guards.

Some retreated into solo pursuits, reading or scratching out correspondence as they idled in their bunks. POWs could send one V-mail letter (maximum twenty-four lines) and one postcard per week to friends and family abroad or to blood relatives in the United States. The quotas for Italian Service Unit members were somewhat looser.

Mail back from Europe, including the occasional package of socks, gloves or cookies, was sporadic at best. When it did come, the salutary effect was immediate. "Nothing improves the morale of these men more than a letter from home," Commander Richter told Charles Marentette for a three-part feature on life at Fort Custer in the *Battle Creek News and Inquirer* in February 1944. "The other day we received approximately 600 letters in one batch, and you never saw a happier bunch of men when [they] were passed out."

A prisoner who did not hear from his family for three months or more was entitled to file an express message with the Red Cross to inquire about their well-being. As conditions in Germany and Italy deteriorated, the odds against getting a response grew long, but not impossible. Richter knew of two internees who had received letters from home after a discouraging span of silence, one of them learning from his wife about the birth of their daughter. "You should see the changes in both of these fellows. They're both pepped up and they are ready to tackle any task they are assigned."

As far as content, Louis Keefer gives us the observations of Ignazio Benfante, manager of a unit at the U.S. Post Office in New York responsible for screening correspondence to and from Italy:

> *In the majority of instances, mail to the prisoners was entirely innocuous, mostly to the effect, "You're lucky to be in America." "Do you need anything?" "We hope to see you."*

> *Early in the war prisoners never sent packages, but received many. The packages were well-scrutinized. If some relative or a friend sent a cake, for example, we'd cut it in half to make sure it didn't contain any weapon. We never found any, but we still had to look.*

Many POWs were complimentary to the United States and said they hoped to remain here. Many southern Italians told relatives that they hoped Sicily would become the forty-ninth state.

"We had to be careful of what we wrote because the mail was censored on both sides," recalled Ernst Floeter. "One side cut out what wasn't allowed, and the other side blacked it out. Sometimes a letter would consist of one big hole."

Mostly young in age and robust in health, prisoners were always looking for ways to discharge their excess physical energy. "They're great hikers, and sometimes walk around the compound for hours at a time," observed a reporter from the *Adrian Daily Telegram* after visiting the sub-camp near Blissfield. "They were the cream of the German army, and the daily exercise helps keep them fit."

Those interested in socializing repaired to the (prisoner-run) PX, where they could redeem their accumulated work compensation (which amounted to up to eighty cents per day) for Cokes, candy, ice cream, razor blades, writing paper and other incidentals. The pocket money was issued as scrip or coupons—no hard currency, which might be used in an escape attempt. Camels, Chesterfields and Lucky Strikes, available at a *Kantine* discount, were used to negotiate favors with the guards. "American cigarets [*sic*] are extremely popular," Major Richter observed. "They buy the most expensive brands of everything."

Few internees exercised their right to put work credits into savings accounts. "'What's the use?' one explained to Marentette. 'If we did try to take it back with us after the war, our own politicians would take it away from us, if you didn't take it away first.' So they carry big fat books of coupons with them, and they buy everything on the PX shelves."

Prisoners were allowed the occasional glass of Michigan wine or up to two bottles of "weak military beer" (3.2 percent alcohol), sold for ten cents apiece at a makeshift bar complete with stools. (Officers were routinely served wine with their meals.) "The Nazis do not like cold beer but drink it at room temperature," Marentette told his readers. Prisoners hoarded and exchanged coupons to get around the limit.

The more entrepreneurial types exploited the market for something stronger than what was officially available, trading grappa, schnapps, moonshine and various fermented brews concocted with the best Old World recipes in stills beneath under the barracks floor. Their customers included the guards as wall as their fellow POWs. Prisoners in the mess kitchen

3.2 beer and Lucky Strikes at the Fort Custer *Kanteen*. *Courtesy of the Historical Society of Battle Creek.*

smuggled out the necessary ingredients for this contraband, including yeast, sugar and dried fruit.

A scene Marentette witnessed at Custer illustrated the power struggles that were conducted over even the smallest aspects of camp life:

> *The superman of the German reich was taking his first crack at good old American gum-chewing when his companions crowded 'round.*

> *"A* Yankee,*" they pointed, accusingly.*

> *He might as well have saluted the Stars and Stripes. The gum was something new and he had tried it, but the experiment was not appreciated by his fellow POWs. They saw in it a softening of this soldier, a tendency to deviate from German ways. And they didn't like it.*

> *He spat the gum on the ground.*

The incident confirmed in microcosm Major's Richter's observation that "[t]hese men don't want to be Americanized in any way." But cracks were bound to show over time.

> *The gum is typical, although since that day several of the more audacious are chewing gum regularly and defying the few who still shout "Yankee" when the offender comes in, jaws working.*

HANSEL AND *GRETEL* AND THE "STREET OF HOPE"

Michigan's POW population had a wide array of recreational options from which to choose, many of them drawing upon talents, vocations and hobbies from their prewar lives. Gardeners cultivated vegetables to enliven the mess table and planted flowers to brighten up the drab landscape. Barracks at Custer competed for beautification prizes.

Plumbers fine-tuned water supply systems, which demanded constant attention. Master mechanics at Camp Evelyn and Au Train in the U.P. repaired logging tools, milling machinery and vehicles. "Not speaking much English," John Pepin tells us, "they would point to pictures of parts they needed to fix the trucks."

Tailors and haberdashers did a brisk business altering and repairing clothing. German cobblers replaced the rubber heels of U.S. Army–issue boots with wooden ones to allow their clients the crisp punctuation expected when saluting officers or executing an about-face. "[They] considered it a matter of pride to be able to snap to attention the way they had been trained," wrote Judith Gansberg. "Many wore wooden sandals on hot days. They weren't very comfortable, but they certainly could click!" Barbers cut hair, often in ways that indicated the prisoner's theater of war. The April 6, 1944 *Enquirer and News* reported that Custer's Afrika Korps veterans favored the "Rommel cut," a style longer than the traditional "Prussian" close-crop adopted as protection from the desert sun.

Camp artisans of all kinds—carpenters, bricklayers, stonemasons, welders, tinsmiths—occupied themselves planning and improving structures, working

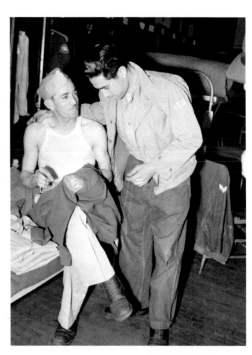

Italians "doing time" at Fort Wayne.
Courtesy of Reuther Archives.

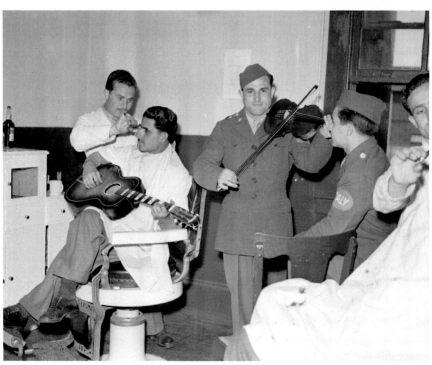

with ingenuity to make the most of the objects at hand. Woodworkers carved plaques, chess pieces, mailboxes (*Briefkasten* to the Germans) and other artifacts, sometimes offering them as keepsakes to friendly Americans, especially youngsters.

As a teenager, Robert Godell was active in the black market that flourished between prisoners and civilians at Camp Sidnaw, and he understood well the value of what was being traded. "Cigars is what they really [prized]," he told Pepin. "They could get cigarettes and all the candy they wanted." Godell swapped a cutting tool with an internee for an Indian head he had fashioned out of the end of an "Upland Pride" orange crate. It was a memento he would cherish for decades.

Camp Lakeview's Gerd Lindeman remembered how the children on the Weick farm were allowed to interact with POWs like they were family. "Matter of fact, the kids were always bouncing around us," he said in an interview with the *Kalamazoo Gazette*. "We had 'em on our backs, horsing around." One day, Lindemann surprised four-year-old Kathleen Weick with a sculpted wooden likeness of, again, an Indian—always a subject of interest to the Europeans. He created it using only a sharpened nail and a razor blade.

Examples of high-quality workmanship abounded in the POW camps. An Au Train internee made a cuckoo clock that kept perfect time for the compound's administration building. Marentette recounted for his readers an example of prisoner folk art that caught his eye during a visit to the Custer commandant's office:

> *On Major Richter's desk is an ashtray supporting a scale model of a German* Stuka *dive bomber made by one of the prisoners from a piece of salvaged pine lumber, an amazingly accurate model complete to a tiny machine gun barrel with a circular wire site protruding from the cockpit hood.*

"The Germans are good craftsmen," Major Richter said as he noticed the reporter's interest in the model. "They [also] like to draw, and have done many fine pictures." The materials, by necessity, were improvised. Some artists appropriated discarded candy boxes from the prison store and drew on the plain cardboard. Disposable, quickly rendered sketches were common, but other works—religious icons, mess hall murals, even (to the dismay of camp personnel) portraits of Hitler—showed more painstaking hours of effort and concentration.

Camp artwork. *Courtesy of MMTHS.*

"Pictures of Rena"

These two pencil sketches came rolled in a tube
marked *"Pictures of Rena by POW"* and
*"Pictures of Renee Kuebler drawn by Prisoners
of War"*
The pictures have different styles and appear to
be signed by different artists but seem to have
been sketched off the same snapshot.
The smaller sketch is dated and inscribed 1944
on the back
The location of the camp it was made in is
unknown

At many camps, prisoners pooled their resources to buy war-surplus projectors and rent films—breezy Hollywood fare showing the United States in the most favorable light. Movie nights were held as often as three or four times a week at Fort Custer, a typical bill including a newsreel, an anti-Nazi *Bugs Bunny* or *Donald Duck* cartoon and an action, comedy or homespun Americana feature. Among the dozens of films he saw during his internment days, Ernst Floeter remembered especially liking *Back to Bataan*, *Abe Lincoln Goes to Washington*, *Edison* and the Hope/Crosby "Road" pictures. Not surprisingly, shows with attractive young women were especially prized. Catcalls and whistles erupted from the audience whenever Dorothy Lamour or Rita Hayworth entered the camera's frame.

The men in the camps enjoyed contact with animals almost as much as they did with children. A group of Fremont prisoners spent hours building an elaborate doghouse for their adopted black terrier pup. POWs at Camp Pori in the U.P. assembled and cared for a small zoo populated with mice, squirrels, goldfish, turtles, snakes and other indigenous creatures. The mascot at Sidnaw was a dog named Smoky, beloved (and very well fed) by internees and guards alike. And prisoners at Au Train adopted deer they saw living in the nearby woods, christening one pair *Hansel* and *Gretel*.

Music was an essential element of doing time in Michigan's POW camps. During the day, prisoners belted out work songs to pass the hours weeding vegetables or felling trees, then continued the practice once back in the compound. They formed glee clubs and staged vaudeville-style revues complete with sets, costumes and donated instruments—shopworn, perhaps, but still serviceable. Again, thanks to the many accomplished artists in their ranks—choirmasters, string and horn players, even the occasional opera singer—the quality was exceedingly high.

In the U.P., Pepin noted the popularity of Camp Pori's sixteen-piece orchestra and Sidnaw's twenty-four-voice choir. In addition to military and administrative personnel, local residents patronized their Sunday-afternoon recitals, held outdoors in the summer. Here is a May 1945 Red Cross report on the scene at Au Train:

> *In addition to the usual carving and painting, the camp has its own orchestral music (3 violins, 1 trumpet, 3 mandolins and 4 guitars) supplemented by recorded concerts (YMCA Concert Record Series) and* Mannerchör *concerts. A few variety shows were also presented during the winter months, written by a professional stage writer.*

Major Richter boasted of the Custer POW who conducted a hotel orchestra in Berlin before entering the German army. The maestro could transcribe by ear the swing and novelty numbers of the day played on radio broadcasts. "The biggest hit so far is 'Pistol-Packin' Mama,'" Richter declared, "though the leader has written a score of his own called 'Coca Cola,' which the men enjoy. It's a cross between a rhumba and bolero, and it is just a jumpy repetition of 'Coca Cola, Coca Cola.'"

"All of the men love to sing," reporter Marentette concluded. "With arms locked together, they sit and mark time by swaying together in a line, singing lustily." Jugglers and magicians were also pressed into entertainment service, as were the two Custer prisoners who had been professional clowns before the war. Their mates donated their canteen coupons to secure the white sheeting they needed for proper costumes.

Kathryn Umphrey remarked on the world the POWs kept hidden from their keepers, the "curious mixture of German humor and customs" she observed during her day at Custer. She conjured a vivid picture for her readers:

> *Viewed during a steady downpour or rain, the camp looked dreary, much as any military post in this country. Occasionally prisoners dashed from one building to another, pausing when confronted by our party to give smartly-executed American salutes.*

> *Some looked surprised at seeing an American woman in the stockade, but most wore the same impenetrable mask they always reserve for American civilians.*

As Umphrey tried to understand how the prisoners "did time," she learned of the existence of one barracks—"the most unusual in the compound"—known throughout the camp as "Wolf's Garden." Most of the men living there had backgrounds in art or theater, and they used those talents to make the spartan surroundings more humane and more bearable.

> *They have their own street signs, which translated read—Border Street, Promenade, Quiet and Still Streets, the Street of Waiting where they line up for daily routine counts, and even a Street of Hope. This last leads to their orderly room where they may make requests.*

> *Day rooms in Wolf's Garden are called "Accademia of Art" and the other a long German name which [a] prisoner [said] was slang and*

not translatable. The nearest he could come to it, he finally decided, was "Boiler Factory."

Inside the boiler factory is an old piano the prisoners have salvaged and a couple other musical instruments. In front of the factory the Germans have constructed what can best be called in English a "joke pole." A short, eight-sided pole, it is used for posting company notices as well as jokes and cartoons.

The barracks resemble those of American troops with a few exceptions— mainly that there are fewer pinup girl pictures and announcements are in both English and German. One of the announcements was an order prohibiting prisoners from hitch-hiking on the post. A few photographs, a picture map of Germany before the war and some woodcuts they have made were on the walls. Here and there were tables they have made from scrap wood and at one of them a prisoner was deeply engrossed with a score of masks he is preparing for the next show.

Wolf's Garden residents organized stage plays and musicals for the camp theater. "We censor the scripts," a Custer official assured Umphrey when he was asked about it. "[O]ne officer is always present at the performance." He recalled that a recent skit imagining eighty-four-year-olds being drafted into the Wehrmacht drew particular belly laughs from those in attendance, Germans and Americans alike.

Readers should not conclude from these examples that "all adherence to [Hitler)] has disappeared," Umphrey warned. "Occasionally a new prisoner still says that he is a Nazi, and a week or so ago when they were ordered to give up all personal effects bearing the swastika or pictures of party members, a sizable number was collected."

Music, vocal and instrumental, solo and in groups, was integral to weekly worship hours, usually conducted by Lutheran ministers or Catholic priests in the area or by chaplains from within the prisoners' own ranks. Attendance was "strong" but by no means universal. "There were always a sizable number…on Sunday, but prisoner life did not seem to induce any men to practice any more conscientiously than they used to in their normal life," Rienhold Pabel recalled of his camp days in Michigan. "[A] great many of Germany's young men" he added, with regret, "had been alienated from the Church even before the advent of Nazidom."

In defiance of their circumstances, almost all prisoners saw holidays as occasions for "lavish" celebration. There was New Year's Eve revelry and an annual Halloween party—like the one planned by the men of Blissfield the day of the train accident. Speeches, ceremony and presents marked every birthday—including the Führer's, which many (secretly) observed together on April 20.

The Easter and Yuletide seasons were especially festive, reflecting the depth of the need to at least partially ward off loneliness and thoughts of family. "From the confines of the German POW camp at Fort Custer float the strains of age-old Christmas carols each evening," reported the *Battle Creek Enquirer and News* on December 22, 1944.

This would be the second time around in captivity for many, and they did everything in their power to import the spirit of their native traditions. At Custer, on the first Sunday of December, "wreaths bearing four electric candles [donated by the International YMCA] were hung in a horizontal position in the center of each barracks," to be lit, one by one each week, as the holiday approached. Stars, garlands, nativity scenes and other handmade decorations adorned forty-foot-tall Michigan evergreens erected in the center of each compound as well as the smaller, indoor trees, purchased by the prisoners.

A fifty-man choir rehearsed a program of song to be performed, with an eighteen-piece orchestra, at the camp theater, the paper reported. Midnight Mass in the chapel (made possible by a waiver of the standard bed-check curfew) promised to draw an overflow crowd. Extra cigarette and food rations, including turkey dinner with all the trimmings, sometimes with Santa Claus himself at the table, also contributed to the desired mood. German bakers in the mess kitchen did their part as well, creating an approximation of *Stöllen*, the loaf-shaped cake so evocative of childhood Christmases.

The YMCA, the Catholic Prisoner of War Fund and other charitable organizations donated reading material for POWs doing time in American camps. The Red Cross shipped crates of books (in German, carefully screened and censored) from Milwaukee to Au Train, along with binding supplies for any necessary repairs. During a stop at the Custer library, Katherine Umphrey saw evidence of the Americanization process dreaded by some in the popularity of Wild West titles. On one shelf there was "even a well-thumbed paperback copy of *See Here, Private Hargrove*," the famously bawdy look at GI life in the U.S. military.

Internees at Custer also had access to the *New York Times, Chicago Tribune* and *Christian Science Monitor.* "The men follow with particular interest the German communiques in the *Times*," Marentette observed, "which they copy and distribute among the companies." The increasingly bad news for the Axis spread quickly and took its toll on morale. According to Commander Richter, "When the British sank the *Scharnhorst*, and when big defeats were reported in Russia, there was a noticeable letdown in the work of the prisoners."

At many camps across the country, POWs created their own newspapers, typically single-sheet fliers filled with amateur poetry, short stories, games, cartoons and puzzles. Italian newsletters had names like *Il Powieri*, *Oltremare* ("Over the Ocean") and *L'Atessa* ("The Wait"). After the German surrender, the editors of the Custer paper changed its name from *Barb Wire* to the more forward-looking *Bridge*. The stock in trade in all of these was irreverent commentary—in the vein of *Private Hargrove*—on the absurdities of the prisoners' daily lives.

Even those with limited English skills studied with care the glossy spreads in *Life*, *Time* and the *Saturday Evening Post*. Besides mining them for the pin-up starlet images (and an occasional photo of Hitler or Göring), they took in with eager eyes images of the material prosperity sure to come once swords could again be beaten into plowshares. In one southwestern desert compound, POWs were permitted to order window curtains from the Sears Roebuck catalogue, but this was unusual. Most camp administrators agreed on the need to keep shopping appetites in check. "The magazines, American ones in particular, have caused a little discontent," Richter confessed in his overview of conditions at Custer. "The men have seen advertisements for watches and clocks and fountain pens and think they can buy them. We had to tell them that they could not."

Men with good conduct records could apply for classes, in subjects that included math and physics, French and English grammar, German literature, American and world history, geography, shorthand and stenography. Most instructors were recruited from local high schools. In some cases, POWs were allowed to enroll in correspondence courses with area colleges. (When Au Train fugitive Verdi of *Wolf's Mouth* arrives in Detroit, the first person he contacts for help is a Wayne State professor from his mail-order English lessons.) There also were prisoner-run workshops in vocations that promised to be in high demand after the war, like mechanical engineering, electrical maintenance and animal husbandry.

IL CALCIO AND THE "CONCHIES"

T hen there were the diversions of competition. Using equipment donated by merchants, church and civic groups and the International Red Cross, POWs embraced almost anything that tested their wits and physical prowess. Most nights in the barracks, one could find men hunkered over chess pieces or checkerboards, throwing dice or tossing cards in rolling games of poker or skat—outlets for the soldiers' universal love of gambling.

Custer's pool cues and ping-pong tables were frayed and worn from heavy use. There is perhaps a bit of stereotyping in Marentette's commentary about table tennis, which opens with the uncontroversial statement that "(t)he life expectancy of a ping-pong ball at a German prisoner of war camp is short indeed."

> *The Nazis, once they get a paddle in hand, are not only experts at the game but play it with a vigor that has amazed American army officers.*
>
> *They ask no quarter from an opponent—and give none—and the ball suffers.*
>
> *"We continually have to replace the smashed celluloid balls," says Maj. E.F. Richter, commander of the camp, explaining that in this game, as in all others, the Germans play with fanatical zeal.*

Cards and pool were popular camp diversions. *Courtesy of the Historical Society of Battle Creek, Reuther Archives.*

"The life expectancy of a ping-pong ball at a German prisoner of war camp is short indeed." *Courtesy of the Historical Society of Battle Creek.*

Outdoor activities were popular, too, regardless of the weather. Fremont prisoners dug a pond off Darling Lake for swimming and bathing on hot summer afternoons. Local children used it, too, for their after-school lifesaving lessons. During the long winter months in the U.P., skiing and snowshoeing were options, as well as contests to build the most creative snowman (or the most curvaceous "snow-woman.") According to Pepin, the POWs at Sidnaw organized a camp Olympics with track-and-field events, including dashes and the high jump. The winners were awarded homemade medals for their efforts.

Boxing (at multiple weight classes) aroused intense interest, as a matter of barracks pride and also as a boon for camp bookmakers, who were more than glad to offer their services to guards and other camp personnel. The Germans played *kegel*, a form of lawn bowling, and the Italians at Fort Wayne had their bocce courts measured out and running within days of their arrival. Baseball never caught on with the prisoners, but volleyball, "fist ball" and "push ball" (rules variable) proved ready and reliable ways to blow off steam.

Most important by far among the POWs' competitive activities was football, European style. No matter how transitory, every compound had

Bare-bones soccer pitch at the Owosso Speedway camp. *Courtesy of the National Archives.*

its pitch, even if it was only a rough clearing in a dirt field. Spectators from around the area gathered to watch the young men run through their paces, still full of energy even after their long workdays. Guards stood at ease along the perimeter, too, and did not flinch if a prisoner climbed the fence to retrieve an errant ball. Lineup spots were hotly contested, and Sunday-afternoon matches, sometimes between camps, were analyzed, discussed and debated all week with the fervency of a religion.

"*Il Calcio*—or, here in the States, soccer—kept Adino and me sane," Verdi recalls of his experience at Au Train.

> *Every day while lumbering, and every night while lying in our bunks, we talked about the team, its strengths and weaknesses, the various plays and strategies we could try. Practice provided a sense of* [liberation] *from the oppression of being a prisoner, and the games often resulted in a most welcome sense of exhaustion, as well as the exhilaration of victory.*

Because of its importance, even this innocent game was not exempt from the power struggles and ideological crosswinds of the camps. In Smolens's novel, the brutal Nazi chieftain Vogel orders reprisals against the Italians—Adino for his talent at scoring goals, coach Verdi for not playing enough Germans.

The natives were invested in the results, too—sometimes for reasons that went beyond the game itself. The charged atmosphere surrounding a Christmas Eve game for Verdi's group, based on real events, offers a striking example. The coach muses to himself:

> *Previously our opponents had been teams from other prisoner-of-war-camps in the Upper Peninsula or northern Wisconsin. But this time we faced Americans. They were prisoners of their own country, and they wore red jerseys with* CO Bombers *hand-painted in white letters on the front.*

The challengers across the field that frigid afternoon were among the few thousand men nationwide granted "conscientious objector" status by their draft boards during the war. Verdi has trouble explaining to his men the concept of "alternative service" for those who, because of religious or moral principles, decline participation in the military. "They don't just *shoot* them?" asks an incredulous Hungarian forward.

These were not even ordinary "conchies." They were disciplinary cases, "incorrigibles" exiled to the "Siberia" of a system of 151 minimum security facilities administered by the Quakers, Mennonites and other "peace churches" across the country. The men of Public Service Camp No. 135, opened in May 1944 near the village of Germfask in the eastern U.P.'s Schoolcraft County, were assigned to build roads, plant trees and make other improvements at nearby Seney National Wildlife Refuge for a token wage of five dollars per month.

Though many doubted the sincerity of the eighty Germfask CO's, it was hard not to be impressed by their credentials. The majority held college degrees, Pepin tells us, and among them were teachers and professors, lawyers and an architect. Decades later, Seney supervisor Harvey Saunders recalled his admiration for one Ivy League–educated prisoner known to all as "Partridge":

> *I got to know him well and, if he hadn't been an objector, one wouldn't want a nicer man. He could speak eight different languages. [H]e firmly believed that the only way they would stop having wars [was] when the man that carried the gun would stand up and say he wouldn't do it.*

Saunders's was a minority view, however. Many local civilians saw the visitors as unwashed and unpatriotic radicals, troublemakers, malcontents— and indeed it seemed their mission to disrupt at every turn. "Potentially, [they had] the makings of a very fine community group, and excellent prospects for self-sufficiency as a work unit," park manager C.S. Johnson wrote in 1947. In practice, however, "these dormant talents were to be exercised in raising hell instead of paying back to the nation the price of escaping military duty." It was not uncommon for a detail of COs to take hours chopping down a tree or sinking a fence post. Even those prone to sympathizing with the objectors grew frustrated over time. "If you handed one a broom and said sweep a platform truck," Saunders remembered, "he would sweep for four hours and the dirt would still be in the truck."

Stories about the conchies' antics dominated talk at Germfask's fire station, diner and barbershop, fueling a slow-boil sense of outrage. People shook their heads in disgust when they heard about internee Corbett Bishop, who, "in the spirit of Gandhi," wore a chain dragging a wooden ball on his leg. They were not surprised when he deserted and, after stops in the Kalamazoo County jail and a correctional facility in Milan, ended up doing time in federal prison.

Germfask Fire Department, 2016. Bad memories of the conscientious objectors of World War II persist in the village even today. *Photo by the author.*

They chafed, too, at what they saw as the COs' abuse of their special privileges, which included permission to leave camp after work on Sundays. Each week, some of the internees on liberty beat a path to Newberry, Grand Marais and other towns in the area, where they took in a movie, bought liquor and consorted with young girls. "The people of Manistique, many of whom had sons and daughters fighting and dying overseas, were angry to see these men and considered them deadbeats," Russell Magnaghi of Northern Michigan University wrote in 1997. "Many had more respect for the German prisoners of war who had fought and were captured than they had for these fellow Americans."

Few mourned when the objectors were transferred to California in 1945 to battle wildfires, ending a 388-day experiment whose bad taste still lingers. On my visit in the summer of 2016, I asked Omar Doran, Germfask's octogenarian manager and unofficial historian, his opinion about the men who lived in the camp so many years earlier. Doran made no effort to hide his disdain for them, and the subject called to mind the day during the war he was called out of his class in grammar school and told his brother had been killed in the Pacific.

This background explains the upside-down scene that unfolds at that Christmas Eve soccer game. The crowd outside the barbed wire cheers for Verdi's POW team while launching insults at the men of other side. Despite their beards and well-earned reputation for disorder, the Bombers prove a formidable opponent that day. In the end, the members of the Au Train team consider themselves lucky to pull out a tie.

PART V

REEDUCATION/REPATRIATION

DEMOCRACY SCHOOLS AND *DER RUF*

E ven as the first shiploads of German and Italian POWs began arriving from North Africa in 1943, thinking was underway about how to get them interested in alternatives to Nazism and Fascism during their captivity. The day would come when these men would return to their homelands, to begin, almost from scratch, the process of rebuilding. It was in our interest that they carry back with them a sense of goodwill about the American people and their democratic institutions.

One step toward making that happen involved simply reminding citizens of the power of their day-to-day interactions. To counter preconceptions of the United States as a soulless, mercenary "haven for lowbrows," a War Department pamphlet offered a checklist of things to avoid bringing up within earshot of the prisoners. Among them: "Careless talk about the uncertainty of the future, our racial problems, our national leaders both civic and military, our relations with the rest of the Allied nations and even the mild complaining most of us do naturally."

In Washington, there was growing support for some kind of crash effort at POW reeducation. A series of (somewhat sensationalized) exposés by Dorothy Thompson and other prominent journalists about bullying and intimidation in the camps caught the eye of Eleanor Roosevelt, who pressed her husband to find a solution to the problem. "I've got to talk to Franklin," the First Lady told an army official over tea at the White House. "Right in our back yard, to have these Nazis moved in and controlling the whole thought process!" The result of this lobbying was the creation of the Special Projects

Division, a unit whose existence was classified because of sensitivity to the Geneva Convention's rules barring indoctrination. According to Ron Robin in *The Barbed-Wire College*, the SPD was set up to pursue its mission "not by psychological manipulation, force, or fear, but through logical persuasion."

The division's multifaceted strategy included traveling classrooms and workshops and the donation of books celebrating America's civic culture to camp libraries. Titles from banned German authors like Heinrich Heine, Thomas Mann and Erich Maria Remarque were also circulated in abundance.

This approach to winning hearts and minds had its doubters. In the October 1, 1944 *Battle Creek Enquirer and News*, Peter Edson wonders whether the sudden availability of material a prisoner may never have seen or heard of before would have any real effect. "He can't be forced to read them—which is the tip-off that ideas can't be forced into anyone's brain if he doesn't want to take them, and the answer to those who would try forced propagandizing." Fort Custer's policy toward those whose resistance took the form of theft or vandalism had his blessing, however. "If a book which Nazis consider dangerous reading should be destroyed by some fanatical prisoner, he pays for another copy to replace it on the library shelves. And so it goes."

By 1945, movie nights for the POWs included fare like Frank Capra's *Why We Fight* as well as newsreels chronicling in detail the collapse of the "Thousand-year Reich." And as the full horrors of the Final Solution were uncovered that spring, administrators made sure the prisoners knew all about them. Documentary footage of death camps was screened in every compound, attendance mandatory. Reactions to what some called *Knöchen* films ("films of bones") ranged from disbelief to outrage and shame. Nazi loyalists predictably dismissed them as "Jewish propaganda."

Anger at the revelations prompted "abrupt changes" in the treatment of PWs, according to Arthur L. Smith Jr. Internees noticed a new coolness in the demeanor of their American custodians. Food rations were shorter and less varied, and rules barring Hitler salutes and swastika flags were enforced with new vigor.

Then there was the so-called Idea Factory at Fort Kearny, Rhode Island, a camp for prisoners specially recruited for their antifascist politics and their writing skills. The men there produced *Der Ruf* ("The Call"), a biweekly newspaper secretly funded under the code name Project Sunflower, sold in canteens across the country for five cents a copy. (Its sponsors understood that free distribution would only fuel the already considerable suspicions potential readers had about its independence.) Columnists and contributors remained anonymous in order to safeguard their families back home from reprisal.

The masthead of the debut issue in March 1945 announces *Der Ruf*'s aims in bold terms:

> *The German Prisoners of War now have their own newspaper!*
>
> [It] *will be way above any party or small group quarrel. It will not serve the personal ambitions of the few. It will foster real German culture. It is the reputation of the German people we have to serve, believing in a sense of goodness and decency.*
>
> *When* Der Ruf *reaches you, answer with a military "Present." Make sure that not one of us who still has a spark of feeling left for home and family is absent.*

Despite the autonomy granted its editorial staff and a circulation that peaked at seventy-five thousand over a twenty-six-issue run, *Der Ruf* failed to achieve traction with its (literally captive) target audience. The rank and file of prisoners found it too academic or literary—and thus too removed from their daily concerns—to warrant serious attention. They preferred instead the jokes and gossip and rundowns of the latest soccer matches offered by the local camp newsletter.

Custer prisoner Elmer Beck offered this post mortem:

> [T]*he Americans wanted us to think in a certain way, to reject our traditional way of life and especially National Socialism. That's why I disliked* Der Ruf. *It was a very disturbing paper for many of us. I know it was written by Germans, but it was filled with propaganda.*

And in spite of official claims of success—hard to measure, in any case—the SPD as a whole must be judged a disappointment as well. Unrealistic aims, clumsy execution and bureaucratic infighting combined with the innate skepticism of the prisoners to render its efforts "manifestly ineffectual," according to Robin. Some internees, eager to turn the page, did try to take in what was being presented to them. Others sought only to game the system, however, enrolling in Civics 101 classes (during which many struggled to stay awake) in the hope that it might move them up in line for repatriation. Surveys of departing prisoners in 1945–46 showed little or no change in attitudes along the lines intended.

The notion of fundamentally reeducating POWs was probably doomed from the start, given the dynamics of camp life. As Robin explained, "The teacher was the warden, and, by implication, he was the enemy. At times the inmate would demonstrate varying degrees of acquiescence; but accepting the worldview of the warden was out of the question." In the blunt words of one German: "I am no longer interested in all of these lectures on democracy. The only thing that interests me is when I can go home and help my family. My wife writes that she and the children are starving."

For all its weaknesses, the SPD may nevertheless have planted at least a few worthwhile seeds. "It cost the government almost nothing," one administrator argued in its defense, "[a]nd many fine people went back to positions in Germany in the media, television, newspapers, politics. I'm sure it couldn't have done any harm, and it probably did a lot of good."

In the end, it was the quality of ordinary interactions with Americans rather than the more artificial measures cooked up in the conference rooms of the Pentagon that won over the prisoners. The Washtenaw County farmer who insisted "No one who works for me eats off a wagon" as he broke bread with them in his soybean field was worth a thousand lectures or newspaper articles. "Experience has shown," the *Enquirer and News* concluded, "that the best line of education is just to let the German prisoners absorb what they can see with their own eyes."

FAREWELL TO THE "LIBERTY STATUE"

THE LONG ROAD HOME

The SPD prepared Germans psychologically for the defeat that ultimately arrived in the spring of 1945. Camp supervisors credited the relatively free access to information it fostered for the generally muted response to news of Allied advances across the Rhine, Hitler's suicide and, on May 8, V-E Day. These big-picture developments triggered sporadic mess hall scuffles around the country, and some openly cried when the end came. But the handwriting had been on the wall for some time, and most prisoners took these developments with stoic passivity or even an exhale of relief. The main concern now—really the *only* one—was how soon they would be going home.

Hopes for a quick resolution to that question were to be dashed. The problem was partly logistics: Washington planners faced too many other pressing issues to make negotiating the mechanics and red tape of the return process a priority. The continuing need for farm labor also factored into what many inside the camps considered unnecessary "foot-dragging." Whatever the reasons, the piecemeal winding-down of America's POW system, for both Germans and Italians, would not be complete until more than a year after cessation of hostilities.

"For days the wildest rumors went around the camp," recalled Konrad Kreitan of that strange and unsettled time after he was transferred from Blissfield to Fort Custer in late 1945.

The optimists said we would be [sent directly] *to Germany. The pessimists pointed out we would be sent to Africa in order to build roads through the desserts* [sic]. *Nobody would know anything exact, until lists of prisoners to be shipped were put on the black board. Here the word* "repatriation" *was used for the first time.*

Kreitan felt lucky the morning in mid-January when his name appeared on the board. There were more trials ahead, but he and the other men providentially selected were on their way, and "moral [*sic*] was correspondingly good."

"One of First PWs at Custer Last to Board Train for Home" reads the headline of a story in the June 22, 1946 *Battle Creek News and Enquirer* about "Hans," a German prisoner preparing to leave Michigan's main base camp. After being drafted into the army, this notably unlikely warrior, a "chubby, rosy-cheeked, blonde Austrian" from the Danube, managed to survive Norway, Finland and Russia before being captured in Tunisia in 1943.

Hans was among a remnant population of about one thousand, many of them transfers from deactivated sites in Illinois and Wisconsin as well as Michigan. Now, at noon on a warm summer solstice Friday, they climbed into the passenger cars of two special trains bound for Camp Shanks on the Hudson River, north of New York City, a main embarkation point for the trip back across the Atlantic. A hospital train would arrive at the Battle Creek station the next day to transport two dozen other Germans east. Three stray Italians, "awaiting hearings in federal court," for reasons unexplained, remained behind.

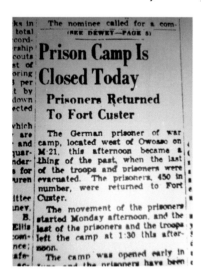

The Owosso Speedway camp is history. *Courtesy of Owosso Public Library.*

In addition to a bedroll, Hans and the others in his group were permitted a barracks bag of up to sixty-five pounds and could wear any portions of their combat uniforms still in their possession. A few were leaving the States, remarkably enough, flush with cash. Uncle Sam made good on the promise of redeeming unused work credits, which in some cases amounted to several hundred dollars— quite a nest egg to take back to war-ravaged Europe.

As he had been an attendant in an American mess hall, the Yanks had taken to calling Hans "Chicken" (in order to

The winding-down of Michigan's camp system was agonizingly slow for prisoners anxious to go home. *Courtesy of the Historical Society of Battle Creek.*

"designate him from the many other Hans at the camp"). His POW buddies adopted the nickname too, which he bore with his usual good humor. His fate now was uncertain. "His parents are dead and he has no brothers or sisters. He has some uncles and aunts, but he hasn't heard from them in several years, and doesn't know if he'll be able to locate them."

If the rules hadn't required that all prisoners be returned to their native countries, Hans—and perhaps many others—might have preferred staying to build a new life. "Fort Custer has been nice," he said, "smiling wistfully" as he boarded, weighted down by the canvas bag over his shoulder.

It was a bittersweet sentiment widely shared. On the eve of their departure, the Custer prisoners staged an international soccer match pitting Germans against Austrians as a kind of goodbye ceremony for themselves and for their American hosts, who clapped, whistled and cheered on the sidelines. Their last job was removing the fences along the camp's western edge. As the trains pulled away, the only signs left of the camp's presence were its guard towers, which post engineers would dismantle within the week.

Four decades later, Konrad Kreitan could recount in detail his last hours on U.S. soil. Attired in newly issued army fatigues and winter hats and coats, "[W]e stood ready," he recalled with emotion in a speech to a Rotary Club audience.

*Each one had in front the seabag filled to bursting, and in the background
the Liberty ship "Code Victory" which was to take us back to the home
country very soon. An American officer held a farewell [speech] in accent
free German. He mentioned the free America and the democracy, which we
should hopefully bring back into post-war Germany. We should not forget
America etc.*

*We were called up each of us by name, placed the ticket around our neck
and went up the gangway to the ship whilst a band played nice melodies.
As a final farewell from America the "Liberty Statue" greeted us at the gate
of the port of New York, and I swore then to come back to this beautiful
America as a free man.*

For many, including Kreitan, the journey home would prove longer and
more circuitous than they could have imagined. It began well. "The return
trip with the ship was quite nice," he recalled of his eight days at sea on the
Code Victory. "We could move freely on the ship, had good food, and even a
cinema on board." The men were given little information about where they
were headed, however, and a new surprise hit them as the ship met landfall.

*[W]e were paniced [sic] when we saw at daybreak on an old, destroyed
water tower in the port the word "Le Havre." We hadn't reached Germany,
but again the French coast.*

After some protest, the prisoners were taken off the ship and transported
to "Phillip Morris," a repatriation camp for American soldiers in Bolbec,
Normandy. Following a quick medical exam, fingerprints and yet more
paperwork, they now found themselves *prisonniers de la guerre,* guarded by
uniformed Moroccan troops with little sympathy for their plight. They were
among the thousands of POWs turned over to the custody of the French
and British—in violation of the Geneva Convention—to serve as labor for
postwar reconstruction.

In his speech, Kreitan did not mince words about his sense of betrayal.
"At that time I swore, we all did it, never again to believe something said by
the Americans. We were fed-up with this so-called democracy."

The conditions in France were harsh—shelters with dirt floors and no
electricity or heat and minimal food. "Now we prisoners, called mockingly
'the Americans,' were first of all subjected to hunger," the daily ration now
"one bread, half a liter of watery soup" and a cup of substitute coffee or

tea. Correspondence was tightly restricted. Kreitan's spirits lifted the day he received a letter from his family, informing him they were alive. Others were not so fortunate. "Their world, kept up with a lot of effort, collapsed like a house of playing cards." Weeks stretched into months, with no sense of when or how their exile would end.

Kreitan did not return home until just before Christmas 1948. He adapted as well as he could to the circumstances, however, and as in America, it was getting to know the natives as *people* that made all the difference. Here are his final touches to the story:

> *The French population accepted us German prisoners of war without any hatred. The morales* [sic] *had changed since 1945 basically. I worked for nearly three years with a French farmer in the Normandy and was treated like a member of the family. Within a hairs breath I nearly married a nice little French girl. My first great love was in France.*

EPILOGUE

"From Enemies to Friends"

We played soccer, we played chess, we had our smokes and we had our beer. It was not a bad time.
—Elmer Beck

"Again we were in the destroyed and hungry Europe of 1946," Konrad Kreitan recalled of the POWs' return after the war. Whether sent directly home or through the unwelcome way station of service in a British or French labor brigade, men like Kreitan, Beck, Gerd Lindemann, Roland Detshel, Eduardo Barbieri and every "Hans" from every camp in the United States came back to a landscape of rubble and extreme privation.

Many wrote letters to their adopted American families to thank them for their treatment and ask for help with the most basic daily necessities. Their friends in Michigan and around the country generously responded, establishing a lifeline of care packages filled with clothing and sewing supplies, shoes, winter coats, soap, chocolates and various canned food items.

As the years passed and the war faded into memory, people on both sides of the Atlantic went about the business of getting on with their lives, and the frequency of the transatlantic exchange naturally tapered off. Many did make an effort to keep in touch, if only with an annual Christmas card, complete with a family photo or two.

A postwar letter of gratitude from Germany. *Courtesy of Houghton County Historical Society.*

Former POWs came back with their wives and children to tour the sites of their wartime internment. Reunions with guards and the families for whom they had once worked were emotional affairs full of laughter, tears and (often colorfully embellished) war stories. Conflicts were airbrushed, with the common theme of letting bygones be bygones. "Luckily one forgets the bad things in life and keeps only the good things in his memory," observed Kreitan, who after his years in France returned to Germany, married his hometown sweetheart and prospered in the candy business.

Kreitan was one of a group of German veterans who offered hospitality to Americans wanting to see the battlefields of their long-ago youth. To his Rotary Club audience, he repeated the words of one prominent visitor, General William "Bill" Douglas of the 102nd Infantry—as a motto for the kind of healing to which men on both sides aspired: "He is a hero who makes his former enemies his friends."

Some ex-prisoners who came back took things further, staying for good. It is hard to know exactly how many pursued citizenship with the aid of an American friend or spouse, but the numbers were substantial, easily in the thousands. Africa Korps captain Lindemann was one such émigré, resettling with his family near Holland, Michigan. Sergeant Beck was another, establishing a life in St. Clair Shores in suburban Detroit.

After several false starts, Ernst Floeter made his return to Michigan in 1957, sponsored by members of the All Saints Episcopal Church in East Lansing. Floeter traveled by train with his wife and infant daughter "on the same route that I had taken as a POW in 1944," he recalls in his memoirs. Within two years, he was earning enough as a photographer to purchase the family's first car, a green 1953 Chevy, worn but serviceable. "We were beginning to live the American dream," he observes with pride.

Soon came the move to Grand Ledge, a town west of the state capital that Floeter and his wife agreed would be a good place to raise the children. "We liked its natural beauty, with the Grand River running through it and sandstone ledges rising up from the banks." Floeter was a model citizen in his new community, active in the chamber of commerce, the Jaycees and the PTA. In 1975, he was named chairman of the city's bicentennial committee—an honor he considered "the highlight of my life."

Barbieri came back to Detroit with his fiancée from Modena and used the skills (and recipes) he had picked up as a mess cook at Fort Wayne to open a restaurant—a business that flourishes today, carried on by his grandchildren.

And, as if to prove the adage "love conquers all," Detroiter Catherine Previdi was able after war's end to make the journey abroad to retrieve her beloved Romano. "Saving up took a year," she remembered of the adventure.

I was one of the last girls in our group who went over to be married, but I said if they could do it, so could I! I sailed on the Sobieski, *a Polish ship, which stopped at Naples, then at Genoa. That's where Romano's brother met me. He then accompanied me during the eight-hour bus ride to Bologna. We were married on 22 November, 1946.*

At first, the parents on both sides withheld their blessing, concerned about the distances involved, geographic and cultural. But the couple was determined to be together. "We enjoyed a brief honeymoon, then I had to come back home to work," Catherine recalled. "I'd taken just a short leave." After two years of delay and plenty of red tape, Romano finally joined his bride in Detroit.

A letter written in halting English by a German who learned to pick apples in Kent County captures nicely the spirit of gratitude most Michigan POWs carried with them after the war, and for the rest of their lives:

> *Surely there were times when the growers could have been accused of fractionalizing [sic] with the enemy. It was a far different country at that time. We were, yet I believe, socially living in what is described as America's melting pot. There were many familiars who had relatives in both Germany and Italy, whom they had been writing and phoning before the war.*
>
> *We were only a couple generation away from the sail boats which brought us here.*

To free up storage space, the U.S. Army destroyed most of its records relating to the POWs in the 1950s, and today there is little physical evidence to remind us of the camps that dotted the Wolverine State during the days of World War II. Libraries and local historical societies do what they can to preserve photographs, news clippings and artifacts, and at the Michigan Military and Technical Historical Society museum in Eastpointe one can see on display a uniform from Fort Wayne bearing the Italian Service Unit insignia. Sketches, jewelry, toys, checkerboards and the like crafted by the prisoners no doubt remain packed away in attic trunks throughout the state.

Armed with maps and metal detectors, amateur archaeologists continue to unearth building foundations, bricks and rusted metal fragments of the barbed wire that once enclosed the men held here. The barracks that housed them were not, for the most part, designed to last, and time and nature have inevitably done their work to reclaim them. On my summer 2016 visit to Sidnaw in the U.P., I had the chance to see a rarity—the camp guard tower, a structure of weathered wood, disassembled into two pieces. It survives as

Remains of Camp Sidnaw guard tower, 2016. *Photo by the author.*

testimony to the ways in which the struggle against fascism reached into the most remote places on the globe.

But much of the remarkable story has been lost. "How could no one mention the German prisoners of war on our farm?" Ron Montri asked in his March 2, 2011 column for the *Monroe Evening News.* When a friend who once worked on the property brought the subject up, Montri recalled feeling as though he had "dropped a bombshell" into his lap.

> *Every family has stories of past generations. My family is no different. But for some reason, no one had ever spoken about the German[s] who picked tomatoes on our farm during World War II. Wouldn't you think the story would have come up some time? [M]aybe when my father or one of his brothers had chugged down a couple of beers?*

"I learned that my great-grandfather didn't trust banks and dug a hole in the floor of his home to hide his money," Montri continued, "but no one mentioned having prisoners of war work in the field under an armed guard just a few hundred yards from the home where I grew up." He used his example to challenge others to pursue their own discoveries.

This page: Twenty-six Germans lie buried in a special section of Fort Custer National Cemetery. *Photos by the author.*

Young Rolf Arnold, one of the Blissfield 16, interred at Custer. *Courtesy of the Historical Society of Battle Creek*

One tangible and particularly poignant physical legacy that remains is the row of twenty-six white headstones in Section B of the Custer National Cemetery, markers for the POWs who died during their internment in Michigan—the sixteen who perished in the Halloween Blissfield disaster and ten others, most of whom died of natural causes. They are among hundreds of prisoners buried at sites all around the United States. In cooperation with the German consulate in Detroit, veterans have gathered there each year since 1953 on the third Sunday of November for formal *Volkstrauertag* ("day of mourning") ceremonies. The bugled taps and the synchronized blasts of rifle salutes echo through the autumn air in remembrance of these forgotten men.

LUNCHTIME ARIA

Of all of the memories Emily Foster shared with me about the Germans who worked on her family's farm during the war, my favorite involved Alphons Schulte, yet another prisoner with talents that went far beyond those required for soldiering. When Emily's father learned, almost by accident, that Alphons had been a concert pianist in civilian life, he invited the man into the house at the end of a lunch break to have a go at the family upright.

His calloused hands had not touched a keyboard in years, but right away, Alphons went through with ease the Schubert and Brahms serenades Emily found so challenging in her after-school lessons. As Mrs. Foster spoke, I saw the same look of awe mixed with envy she must have displayed when those notes first poured from his fingers.

As the harvest weeks passed, more glittering, impromptu concerts followed. The audience—Alphons's fellow POWs, perched on crates outside, listening through the open window, as well as Emily and the other members of the Teichman family, seated with the guard around the kitchen table—came to expect them as a kind of post-meal ritual. And despite Hitler's decree that only German music be played in the Reich, Alphons proved himself fluent with composers from other countries, too, executing their works with just the right balance of pace, technique and feeling. "What he could *do* with Chopin!" Emily declared, still moved by the thought of it so many years later.

The author with Emily Foster in her home, 2016. *Photo by the author.*

One day, as Alphons entered through the front door and took his usual place at the piano bench, another prisoner, known to his mates for his trained tenor voice, rose to his feet and ascended the steps to the porch, to a spot next to the window. As the musician began to play, the singer closed his eyes, gathered himself and then put body and soul into an aria from Puccini's *La Bohème* (probably "Che Gelida Mamina"—"What a Cold Little Hand").

The Germans and Americans present took it all in, spellbound. Just as it was with the Sunday band concerts at Camp Sidnaw, the "Ave Maria" performed at the funeral for the Blissfield 16, the carols sung at Custer's midnight Christmas Masses and the Sparta POW "whose voice would take over and tear your heart out," the war, for a moment, melted away, as did any inhibitions about "fractionalizing" with the enemy. Lost in their private thoughts, humbled by the power of art and the solace of mutual friendship, several in the little improvised community wiped tears away as the performance concluded. Then they readied themselves for another afternoon, among trees heavy with ripened Michigan fruit.

SELECTED BIBLIOGRAPHY

Atkinson, Rick. *An Army at Dawn: The War in North Africa, 1942–1943.* New York: Simon and Schuster, 2002.

Calamandrei, Camilla. *Prisoners in Paradise.* Documentary, 1990.

Carlson, Lewis H. *We Were Each Other's Prisoners.* New York: Basic Books, 1998.

Crowley, Betty. *Stalag Wisconsin: Inside WWII Prisoner-of-War Camps.* Oregon, WI: Badger Books, 2002.

Floeter, Ernst W. *I'll See You Again, Lady Liberty: The True Story of a German Prisoner of War in America.* Livermore, CA: WingSpan Press, 2014.

Galbraith, Mary. "Sparta, MI German POW Camp." *Military History of the Upper Great Lakes*, October 14, 2016.

Gansberg, Judith M. *Stalag, U.S.A.: The Remarkable Story of German POWS in America.* New York: Thomas L. Crowell Company, 1977.

Garcia, J. Malcolm. "German POWs on the American Home Front." *Smithsonian*, September 15, 2009, https://www.smithsonianmag.com/history/german-pows-on-the-american-homefront-141009996.

Hall, Kevin T. "The Befriended Enemy: German Prisoners of War in Michigan." *Michigan Historical Review* (Spring 2015): 57–79.

Keefer, Louis E. *Italian Prisoners of War in America, 1942–1946: Captives or Allies?* New York: Praeger, 1992.

Krammer, Arnold. *Nazi Prisoners of War in America.* New York: Scarborough House, 1996.

Leibowitz, Liel, and Matthew Miller. *Lili Marlene: The Soldiers' Song of World War II.* New York: Norton, 2009.

Mallet, Robert. "Germans in the Onions." *South Bend Tribune*, January 8, 1978.

Marsh, Melissa Amateis. *Nebraska POW Camps*. Charleston, SC: The History Press, 2014.

Mencarelli, John. "Our Little-Known POW Camps." *Detroit Free Press*, January 5, 1975.

———. "The Peach Ridge POWs." *Grand Rapids Press*, September 15, 1974.

Miller, Duane Ernest. "Barbed-Wire Farm Laborers: Michigan's Prisoner of War Experience During World War II." *Michigan History* (September-October 1989): 12–17.

Pabel, Reinhold, *Enemies Are Human*. Philadelphia: John C. Winston Company, 1955.

Pepin, John. *The Enemy in Our Midst*. Documentary, with Jackie Chandonnet. WNMU-TV, 2004.

———. "POW Camps in the U.P." *Marquette Mining Journal*, January 2001.

Peterson, Michael. "Bound by Her Secret History." *Owosso Argus-Press*, January 19, 2010.

Pieti, Jacob. "Sidnaw, MI WWII POW Camp." *Military History of the Upper Great Lakes*, October 11, 2015.

Robin, Ron. *The Barbed-Wire College: Reeducating German POWS in the United States During World War II*. Princeton, NJ: Princeton University Press, 1995.

Smith, Arthur L., Jr. *The War for the German Mind: Re-Educating Hitler's Soldiers*. Providence, RI: Berghahn Books, 1996.

Smolens, John. *Wolf's Mouth*. East Lansing: Michigan State Press, 2016.

Sumner, Gregory D. *Detroit in World War II*. Charleston, SC: The History Press, 2015.

Thompson, Antonio. *Men in German Uniform: POWS in America During World War II*. Knoxville: University of Tennessee Press, 2010.

Van Roekel, John. *Prisoner Moon*. Charleston, SC: Createspace, 2012.

WPA American Guide Series. *Michigan: A Guide to the Wolverine State*. New York: Oxford University Press, 1941.

INDEX

ABOUT THE AUTHOR

Gregory D. Sumner is co-chair of the Department of History at the University of Detroit Mercy, where he has taught since 1993. Sumner holds a PhD in American history from Indiana University and a JD from the University of Michigan Law School. His previous books include *Unstuck in Time: A Journey through Kurt Vonnegut's Life and Novels* (Seven Stories Press, 2011) and *Detroit in World War II* (The History Press, 2015).